AF340694

THE PEARL NECKLACE

To Susan,

this necklace
with beads
of friendship

Roberto

apr/92

AWARDED THE 1991 HOWER PRIZE

THE PEARL NECKLACE

Toward an Archaeology of Brazilian Transition Discourse

ROBERTO REIS

Translated by Aparecida de Godoy Johnson

University Press of Florida
Center for Latin American Studies
Gainesville Tallahassee Tampa Boca Raton Pensacola Orlando
Miami Jacksonville

Cover photo courtesy of Tatiana Chagas Memória, director, Museu da Imagem e do Som, Rio de Janeiro.

Library of Congress Cataloging-in-Publication Data

Reis, Roberto.

The pearl necklace : toward an archaeology of Brazilian transition discourse / Roberto Reis; translated by Aparecida de Godoy Johnson.

p. cm.

Includes bibliographical references and index.

ISBN 0-8130-1105-1

1. Brazilian prose literature—20th century—History and criticism. 2. Brazilian prose literature—19th century—History and criticism. 3. Modernism (Literature)—Brazil. 4. Literature and society—Brazil. I. Title.

PQ9603.R38 1992

869.8—dc20

91-23277

CIP

The University Press of Florida is the scholarly publishing agency for the State University System of Florida, comprised of Florida A&M University, Florida Atlantic University, Florida International University, Florida State University, University of Central Florida, University of Florida, University of North Florida, University of South Florida, University of West Florida.

Orders for books should be addressed to:
University Press of Florida, 15 Northwest 15th Street, Gainesville, FL 32611.

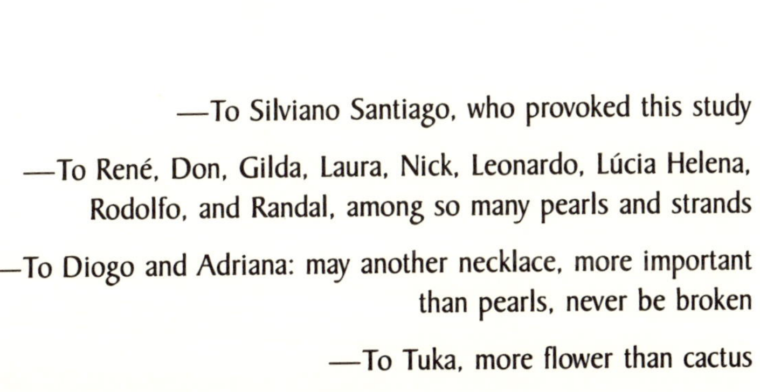

—To Silviano Santiago, who provoked this study

—To René, Don, Gilda, Laura, Nick, Leonardo, Lúcia Helena, Rodolfo, and Randal, among so many pearls and strands

—To Diogo and Adriana: may another necklace, more important than pearls, never be broken

—To Tuka, more flower than cactus

Contents

Acknowledgments

Much of the material in this book has been published or presented elsewhere. An earlier version of "The Mask and the Face" appeared in *Quadrant* 6 (1989): 59–80, published by the Centre de Recherche en Littérature de Langue Portugaise of the Université Paul Valéry, Montpellier III (France). A portion of the chapter was presented at the XIV International Congress of the Latin American Studies Association, New Orleans, March 1988. The section on *Don Quijote* appeared in an abbreviated version in *Minas Gerais* (*Suplemento Literário*), 4 August 1984.

"The Self-Portrait and the Back of the Portrait" originated in a lecture delivered in the Department of Spanish and Portuguese, University of Minnesota, in February 1986. A slightly different version has appeared in *Estudos* 6 (1987): 85–103, a publication of the Federal University of Bahia.

"The Carpenter of Letters" reproduces, with some modifications, a critical study included in the volume on Humberto de Campos, titled *O miolo e o pão* (Niterói/Brasília: Universidade Federal Fluminense/Instituto Nacional do Livro, 1986), 39–50, which I edited for the Brazilian Instituto Nacional do Livro. A summary of the text was presented at the Cincinnati Conference on Romance Languages and Literatures, University of Cincinnati, 1987.

"The Almond Tree and the Banana" has been published in the *Revista Interamericana de Bibliografía* XXXIV, 2 (1989): 169–76, a journal published by the Organization of American States.

"The Narrow Limits" was published in *Brasil/Brazil*, 5, 4 (1991): 39–53.

A condensed version of "The Pearl Necklace" was presented at the Tenth Symposium on Portuguese Traditions, UCLA, April 1987, and will be published in *Ibero-Americana Pragensia* XXIV.

"All History Is Remorse" was delivered as a lecture at the University of Texas at Austin in April 1989 and was published in *Ideologies & Literatures* 4, 1 (1989): 149–65. The text benefited greatly from the dialogue with students in my graduate course on Carlos Drummond de Andrade in the Fall of 1988 in the Department of Spanish and Portuguese, University of Minnesota. For this, I am extremely grateful for the stimulating intellectual presence of Dário Borim, Josephine Books, José Cerna, Ramón Figueroa, Paul Larson, Jorge Vidal, Jason Wood, and José Mauro Zonis.

A slightly different version of "The Map of the Map-of-the-Map" has appeared in *Chasqui* XVII, 1 (1989): 10–16.

My sincere thanks to the editors of the journals mentioned for their authorization to include the essays in this volume.

I would like to thank the Department of Spanish and Portuguese of the University of Minnesota for the logistical support and incentives which have been indispensable for the elaboration and publication of this book, and the College of Liberal Arts, which, in the form of a single quarter leave, allowed me to complete the manuscript. I would also like to acknowledge the assistance of the Inter-Library Loan staff of the Wilson Library. Colleagues such as David William Foster, Lúcia Helena Costigan and, particularly, Randal Johnson, were constant and tireless interlocutors of the ideas outlined in this study. Rodolfo Franconi, René Jara, Silviano Santiago, and Marisa Lajolo must be recognized for having read the manuscript. I am also grateful to James Romano, Leonardo García, and Donald Ramos who helped in the final stages of elaboration, and to Roberto Acízelo Quelha de Souza and Laura Padilha, who helped with bibliographical references. I must also recognize the efforts of Antonio Ramos-Gascón and Connie Weil, as well as those of Aparecida de Godoy Johnson, who deserves special thanks for translating the book.

I wish to thank the members of the Hower Prize Committee of the Center for Latin American Studies, University of Florida, and to Phillip Martin, Walda Metcalf, and Teresa Jesionowski, from the University Press of Florida—my first editors in a language other than my own—for their competence and understanding.

No words would be sufficient to express my gratitude to Nicholas Spadaccini, who frequently endured my impatience about seeing the book in print, especially when crucial decisions depended on third parties. And finally to Antonia, Diogo, and Adriana, my love, once again, for having tolerated so many hours of my absence and so many flights of imagination in the process of researching, thinking through, and writing this book.

Foreword

In the last few years Roberto Reis has become a major voice in the study of Brazilian literature in the United States. Prior to moving to this country in 1986 to assume a position at the University of Minnesota, he received his Ph.D. from the Universidade Católica in Rio de Janeiro and taught at several Brazilian universities. In Brazil he published a collection of short stories, a novel, and numerous critical studies, including the book *A permanência do círculo* (1987). *The Pearl Necklace*, winner of the University of Florida's Center for Latin American Studies 1990 Alfred Hower Prize, is his first book published in the United States.

The Pearl Necklace is a polemical and in many ways provocative study of Brazilian literature that goes against the grain of dominant critical approaches and interpretations. As a means of avoiding periodization hypotheses based on a progressive succession of literary themes and styles, Reis focuses on what he broadly defines as the period of *transition* that goes from around 1850, when slave traffic was abolished, to approximately 1950, when the process of industrialization rapidly increased. During this long time frame Brazil underwent a process of modernization and was transformed from an essentially agrarian society ruled by landed elites to an increasingly urban society with a much more complex social structure.

Pursuing the line of research begun with *A permanência do círculo*, where he critically examined such writers as José de Alencar, Cyro dos Anjos, Lúcio Cardoso, and Autran Dourado, in *The Pearl Necklace* Reis argues that throughout the transitional period, and perhaps even until today, Brazilian literature has been marked by a discourse homologous to the country's hierarchical, elitist, authoritarian, and closed social structure. His analysis explores, and ultimately rejects, a notion frequently employed in Brazilian criticism, that is, that literature has been a force for ideological transformation and transgression. Reis reveals instead that many works either replicate the social order or symbolically reconstruct it on the level of the imaginary.

Through readings of such writers as Humberto de Campos, José Lins do Rego, Galeão Coutinho, Carlos Drummond de Andrade, and Graciliano Ramos, Reis suggests that much Brazilian literary production—even much of that ostensibly on the left—rests on a conservative substratum that contributes to the perpetuation of unjust and closed structures of power. He argues that Brazilian literature only rarely admits the voice of the Other or recognizes the alterity of difference. Literature itself, furthermore, seldom questions language as an instrument of power or the role and function of literature as a social institution. Among writers studied in this volume, Reis makes exceptions only for those whose literary practice fractures the monolithic solidity of discursive certainty, such as Machado de Assis and the Érico Veríssimo of *O tempo e o vento*, whose critical questioning of language ties them to writers such as Oswald de Andrade, João Guimarães Rosa, and Clarice Lispector.

Reis's book points toward the need for new strategies in the study of Brazilian literature, moving away from a charismatic and essentialist vision of writers and their work and a predominant focus on the internal analysis of individual texts, which have come to constitute what Pierre Bourdieu calls the "professional ideology" of literary critics everywhere. He argues for a socio-critical approach that situates literature, literary practice, and literary producers (*qua* intellectuals) in the social, political, and institutional frameworks which authorize, empower, and legitimize them. He calls, in short, for analysis of the relationship between literature and diverse levels of authority and power in Brazilian society.

By rejecting what has been called the "tyranny of the text," grounding literary practice in broader social and historical currents, and viewing literature as one social discourse among others with equal claims to legitimacy, Reis participates in an ongoing process of the reevaluation of the Brazilian literary canon, itself a structure of authority in the cultural field. In this sense, his study laudably includes writers who have been virtually ignored by Brazilian criticism—Humberto de Campos and Galeão Coutinho—and examines canonical authors (Lins do Rego, Drummond, Graciliano Ramos) from a new and unorthodox perspective.

Readers may well take issue with a number of questions the book raises, with aspects of its conceptual framework, or with some of its conclusions—the admittedly "porous" notion of *transition,* the author's rather unforgiving attitude toward much literary memorialism, the failure to include women writers in the analysis, the normative coloration of many of the analyses—but the author's intention is precisely to open a dialogue on the critical questions facing Brazilian literature today. With *The Pearl Necklace,* Reis seeks to incite debate, to provoke responses, to initiate discussions with as many interlocutors as possible about the particular literary and social issues it raises. One can only hope that readers and other critics will respond to the challenge.

Randal Johnson
University of Florida

THE PEARL NECKLACE

Historical society, in the strong sense of the term,
is that which is not in history, but rather
that for which having a history and being
in history is a problem.

—*Marilena Chauí*

Case

Every text opens to or, as Derrida would have it, "breathes" other texts, and this one is no exception, since it strolls, openly or in a more disguised fashion, through many other texts. One of its more important dialogues is with some of my own previous work, especially *A permanência do círculo.* When I finished it in 1983, I had no intention of continuing that line of research, but subsequent reading reaffirmed and reinforced the interpretation advanced at that time. Fortuitous circumstances then led me to turn toward the book I now begin, which attempts to weave studies written between 1986 and 1988 into a more or less organic and harmonious whole.

My intention is to contribute in some way to a history of Brazilian literature during what I call, fully aware of the expression's precariousness, a period of *transition* extending from approximately 1850 until around 1950, focusing more specifically on the narrative of the 1930s. It is a history, however, that is purposefully fragmentary and unfinished, not only because it would be beyond my reach to exhaust the material but also because I hope to avoid the (false) pretension of totality and completeness that characterizes so much literary historiography. Rather, I want to emphasize that this study is a gesture that seeks to open areas of research, sketching a mosaic of an unwritten history, a mural, and a sphinx awaiting a more satisfactory deciphering by future scholars.

Second, most available histories of Brazilian literature tend to transform the 1930s into a list of isolated authors, who may be examined in greater or lesser detail, but without a full rendering of the social and ideological background underlying the decade's fictional production and without articulating it with other cultural manifestations or even other writers of the period. In other words, the necessary contextualization tends to be lost, a situation aggravated by the fact that when most literary histories discuss Modernism, they tend to see the movement as the "resolution" of all the impasses and contradictions faced by previous literary currents as well as of Brazilian society as a whole. We thus need to rethink both the strategies used to analyze the 1930s and the institutionalized interpretation of Modernism that dominates Brazilian literary criticism today.

This leads me to another vector guiding this book: the problem of canonization. Much remains to be done in Brazilian criticism. It is imperative to reread the established canon from a different perspective, one more concerned with the social and the historical than with the aesthetic, especially since our historiography clearly privileges the criteria of "period styles." It is equally important to read neglected or "minor" authors and texts and to work with forms that orthodox, immanent modes of criticism consider "nonliterary," such as memoirs, lyrics of popular music, cordel poetry, and other cultural manifestations outside the elitist circuit of Brazilian literature. Moreover, it is crucial to question the complex process of production, circulation, reproduction, and reception of the cultural artifact.

The critic interprets discourses, and literature is but one among many discourses deserving our attention. Even if we think in strictly literary terms, figures of the importance of Machado de Assis require both new exegeses of consecrated texts, in accordance with different *ways of reading*, and an examination of genres considered "secondary," such as crônicas (short, journalistic vignettes based on events of everyday life), which are today almost forgotten.

This study thus includes discussions of less-known authors (Humberto de Campos and Galeão Coutinho), less frequently analyzed genres (memoirs), periods which have only recently begun to attract the attention of critics (such as the belle époque), and less-studied texts by consecrated authors (such as José Lins do Rego's *Eurídice*). At the same time, it undertakes rereadings, from new angles, of renowned writers (Alencar, Machado, Érico Veríssimo, Drummond) and literary movements (Modernism). These analyses emerge through a focus on Modernism and the 1930s, both included in the period of *transition* that I propose as an alternative to escape from periodization according to literary style.

The introductory chapter, a "first strand," should be seen as a horizon above which the remaining chapters orbit. In them the reader will find some inevitable repetitions, which I have chosen to maintain so as to preserve each chapter's autonomy and internal coherence. The idea is that the studies—loose beads strung on a single thread—will have a meaning of their own and will also enter into dialogue with each other, weaving a story pointing toward a history of the Brazilian *transition* as defined in the first chapter.

Central issues of this history include the authoritarian undercurrent of Brazil's cultural discourse; the contradictory profile of the country's modernization; the role of intellectuals, often co-opted in the construction of a strong, centralized State; and the aversion toward History that seems to characterize the Brazilian social formation. In such a context, it becomes difficult to analyze literature in terms of transgression. Also important is a rethinking of the historicization of authors, works, and genres in such a way as to fracture the canon as a closed, elitist structure. In sum, condensing my concerns into an incisive assertion: History must be taken *as a problem*.

Besides this, it seems imperative to attempt to grasp the literature of the period emphasized here more in terms of a *discursive pattern* than within the limits of a strict chronology. In other words, books and writers that belong to or were published during the 1930s present certain thematic invariables or an ideological profile that can be detected in texts and authors who reveal identical or similar postures but whose works were either not published during that decade or who are not usually included in the so-called second modernist moment by traditional historiography. I am thinking, to give but one example, of a novel such as Lúcio Cardoso's *Crônica da casa assassinada,* published in 1959 but which perfectly fits the predominant tendencies of the 1930s. This study seeks to outline the contours of what one might call the fictional discourse of the period of *transition,* and it is in this sense, without rigid chronological limits, that references to the 1930s should be understood throughout the chapters that follow.

This is a book of literary criticism. As I am concerned with a sociohistorical approach, I have invaded areas such as history, political science, anthropology, sociology, in an interdisciplinary strategy. I hope that scholars from these disciplines will forgive me for this intrusion and for any misinterpretations I may have made when attempting to outline an authoritarian discursive pattern.

Minneapolis,
October 1988
(Revised—Brooklyn Park,
November 1990)

First Strand: The String

The Mask and the Face

And if now I look through my already numerous works, which represent a lifetime, I do not see myself even once grab the mask of time and slap it as it deserves. At best I made a few faces from afar.
—*Mário de Andrade*

I suppose that all writers have a manuscript in a drawer that will never see a typesetter. No exception, several years ago I wrote a book of a theoretical nature in which I attempted to delineate the *place of literature,* arguing that the literary text coexists in cultural space with other discourses from which it absorbs traces, in such a way that one can read the context (that is, a set of texts) through the literary text. At this time, I am not interested in pursuing that argument, which I subsequently synthesized in other works, but the study gave rise to a question that has intrigued me for some time.[1] In that forgotten essay, I understood literature as a form of *transgression:* as a representational discourse, literature placed social interdictions in parentheses and scoured possibilities of the real behind the appearance of reality that surrounds and limits us. Such an understanding, some ten years ago, led me to conceive of the fantastic as an extremely subversive language.

After the publication of my theoretical speculation was frustrated, I began to study Brazilian literature more systematically and to confront certain difficulties in applying the same notion to the Brazilian literary text. In a way, this book attempts to outline an explanatory hypothesis. It would thus be appropriate to begin, even if only schematically, by exploring some of the problems involved in seeing the literature produced in Brazil, in its most general contours, as transgressive. But first, as a means of initiating the discussion, I will briefly examine, with no pretense of providing a detailed panorama of Brazilian history, the fundamental characteristics of what I call *transition.*

Numerous scholars of the Brazilian social and cultural formation have pointed out its authoritarian nature. Marilena Chauí writes that Brazilian society is authoritarian, "since at the threshold of the twenty-first century it has been unable to realize even the centuries-old principles of liberalism and republicanism" (*Conformismo e resistência,* 47).[2] In effect, from the colonial period until the present one can detect flagrant authoritarianism in the Brazilian sociocultural fabric. Roberto Ventura observes that "the colonization of Latin America, starting in the sixteenth century, constituted a military, commercial, and religious operation implying a scriptural enterprise. Writing, describing, translating, and interpreting are some of the operations involved in taking power in a territory belonging to others" (1). It would not be difficult to show how a majority of texts about the other imply an intent to dominate. In the colony Portugal implanted a system completely outdated in Europe (Iglésias, *História e ideologia,* 68–69). If one can appreciate the efficacy of Portugal's monstrous state machinery, to the extent, for example, that it was able to preserve territorial unity, one must at the same time recognize its authoritarian character. In the words of Laura de Mello e Souza, "The State was one of the supports of the colonial system's political economy—an absolutist State which, as such, could not exist without multiple facets of power and violence: administrative centralism, taxation, and the arbitrary actions of rulers and potentates" (99).

As we know, Independence (1822) was a movement in which landed seignorial sectors played a key role, and the nineteenth century witnessed the consolidation and decline of their hegemony. A comparison of the social and historical conditions underlying European romanticism with those of Brazil is revealing. According to José Guilherme Merquior, "Culturally, the two essential characteristics of nineteenth-century Europe were the universalization of the bourgeois life-style—the economic, political and *cultural* predominance of middle sectors—and, toward the middle of the century, the generalization of forms of behavior introduced by the growth of cities, or, the increasingly *impersonal* and atomistic character of human relations in the large demographic concentrations" ("Situación del escritor," 375).

European literature moves through these themes: the repudiation of the "gray life" and prosaic nature of the quotidian, accompanied by criticism of the process of dehumanization in the large metropolis. With its reactivation of religion through the cosmic expansion of the self, romanticism combats the banalization of bourgeois experience, just as postromantic art defends the spirit against the erosion of experience in the contemporary urban-industrial world (375).

The universalization of the bourgeois ethos and the consolidation of the large city are directly linked, according to Merquior, to the Industrial Revolution, which would not have occurred without a high level of economic differentiation in eighteenth- and nineteenth-century European society. In Latin America, however, middle sectors were small, markets incipient, and the process of industrialization practically nonexistent. Large urban concentrations were slow in developing, and the universalization of the bourgeois ethos was blocked by the survival of seignorial customs and traditional modes of behavior (376). The result was that in nineteenth-century Latin America romanticism's "critical" literature was "committed above all to the ideal of modernization of society (that is, *bourgeoisement* and industrialization), while in Europe it was a countercultural style committed to a critique of the *consequences* of that very same modernization" (377).

In Brazil an identical divorce between sociohistorical reality and cultural life occurred. We imported liberal and romantic ideas, which fluctuated on being transplanted to a still provincial milieu, displaced and "misplaced" in a slaveholding society, which had never experienced anything analogous to the French or Industrial Revolutions. This displacement has been acutely analyzed by Roberto Schwarz, who sees in nineteenth-century Brazil an oblique relationship, a true cultural whiplash, between the social context and its literary translation. Such a frankly ideological representation served to shore up the dominance of the landed elites, producer and consumer, in the final analysis, of the literature that was written and read during the period. As I have attempted to show in another study, the concept of "nationalism" forged by Brazilian romanticism attended to the interests of this group, which was practically isolated in power after Independence and which needed a heroic, legendary, and mythical past that would cement its hegemony.[3]

Renato Ortiz has suggested that imported ideas eventually acquire a legitimizing function, on the one hand, justifying the implantation of the Republic and, on the other, attempting to solidify a conception of the Brazilian State as a goal, which will occur in the 1930s (30–31). With the improvement of capitalism in Brazil, such ideas tend to "move into place," making our class structure equal to that of other capitalist societies (106).

Discussing, like Ortiz, Schwarz's polemical *Ao vencedor as batatas,* J. Guilhon de Albuquerque proposes a correction in the concept (implied, in his view, in Schwarz's introductory chapter) of the transition of an estate-based social structure toward a more characteristically mercantile and bourgeois order, replacing it with the concept of contradiction. In this case, Albuquerque writes, "The obstacle to understanding nineteenth-century Brazil would not be in wanting to explain the passage from a seignorial (traditional) society to a mercantile (modern) society (as European political and literary thought formulates its own history) since what we have is a society which is contradictory from the outset, in which seignorial classes are simultaneously mercantile and modernizing, in which the amenities of a liberal façade rest on the solid foundations of compulsory and semicompulsory work, and in which law is accommodated with a patronage system" (57). In later essays, Schwarz defends his arguments and extends them to the present.[4] Albuquerque's correction seems pertinent, however, and I would elaborate it by bringing the fundamental ambiguity of the Brazilian social formation into the debate.

The moments of crisis in Brazilian history have always provoked epidermic changes but have left the pillars of the social edifice practically untouched. Independence did not extinguish slavery; Abolition merely led to the metamorphosis of the slave into the black worker in a class society; the Republic did not extirpate rural oligarchies; 1930 resulted in one more rearrangement of the ruling classes in power. If we examine the Brazilian past, we see a country that was an agro-exporting colony which is now the world's eighth largest economic power. Nevertheless, Brazil still has huge disparities and contradictions to be solved.

What is in question here is to underline this fundamental duality between surface and depth, in which the binomial transition/contradiction is interwoven, the first term corresponding to the more external facets while the second would be more deeply rooted, starting with the country's adoption of an economic and cultural model that, on one hand, was a consequence of the expansion of capitalism but, on the other, has many similarities with a social system already somewhat outdated in seventeenth-century Europe. In this sense, Brazil's social formation has always evolved by conserving its contradictory nature, undertaking, however, a shift from a seignorial and patriarchal model to an industrial one in which the landed hegemonic social group ceases to be the exclusive occupant of the seat of power, without being totally dislodged from power, which now has to be shared with fractions of the bourgeoisie.

One must always keep the peculiar characteristics of the Brazilian bourgeoisie in mind. It cannot be understood in classical terms, for it did not dispute political power with an aristocracy, since such an aristocracy has never existed in the country; it does not aspire to hegemony, since it effectively exercises it; it does not desire to restructure the social order in a revolutionary fashion, since the existent order fits its purposes; it does not oppose foreign capital, because its prosperity and modernity derive from its alliance with foreign capital. One may thus conclude that it is in the bourgeoisie's interest both to maintain links of dependency (instead of overcoming them) and to perpetuate the old order (instead of transforming it) (Ribeiro, 96). Such a profile is essential for an adequate understanding of the pact of 1930 and the country's problematical modernization.

The industrializing State faces difficulty in its own formation not only because oligarchical groups retained power until 1930 but also because neither urban middle sectors, incipient industrial groups, nor the military were able to formulate satisfactorily an alternative proposal. This will only happen later on, by benefiting from the critical international conjuncture detonated in 1929. Only "after the 1937 coup does the Army begin to constitute a sort of single party, providing guidelines of conduct for the industrializing State," acting, in the period from 1939 until 1945, as "a true center of aggregation for the interests of the urban middle sectors" (Saes, *Classe média e política na Primeira República*, 108). Such an alliance, between the military and entrepreneurs committed to associated multinational capital, and counting on the support of intermediate sectors in large cities, will recur with complete success in the seizure of power in 1964.

If we keep this trajectory in mind, we can see that it is characterized by the predominance, on the discursive level, of an authoritarian model that impedes the *difference* that had hoped precisely to assure the sector's hegemony. Such a discourse is directed toward the constitution of the Brazilian State, which has been an ambition of intellectual elites since at least the nineteenth century. A number of elements converge in this project: the adoption of scientism,[5] of naturalism in literature,[6] the "purifying" intervention of hygienist physicians,[7] the racial policy of whitening the population (visible in the stimulus given to European immigration to substitute the labor force composed of black slaves), aryanism in the cultural sphere (which rejected popular manifestations),[8] public sanitation, and Pereira Passos's campaign for urban renewal. On the other hand, in both the political/ideological and cultural spheres, this discourse is frequently dressed in nationalist clothes and expresses a localism/centralism dichotomy.

Emphasizing that Brazil is a country with a long authoritarian tradition, Simon Schwartzman attributes the origins of Brazilian authoritarianism to the "models of relationship between State and society" (9). Brazilian politics have always been based on a patrimonial system, a form of domination in which there are no well-defined boundaries between the public and the private. The elites who achieved the country's emancipation from Portugal—which could be understood as an initial thrust toward the institutional modernization of a country until then stifled by its colonial status—entered the nineteenth century (the age of liberalism) politically and economically dependent, subordinated to both Portugal and to England and establishing a model inherited from the colonial period characterized by a bureaucratic centralization to administer a declining economy (Schwartzman, 43, 86).

Consequently, it is important to reemphasize that the unfolding of the Brazilian political process in the direction of a modern State (transition) has always been undermined by the contagion of vestiges of the most retrograde and conservative elements of that which it attempted to dissipate. Schwartzman further emphasizes this ambiguity by showing that the political theses of centralization (that is, the vector favoring transition) and decentralization (that is, the vector that would favor the preservation of tainted local bossism) are poorly formulated, since what occurred was not merely one of these things, but rather both: "on the one hand, a centralized and hierachical political power that did not depend on local bases of support, but rather on its own governmental machine to be able to subsist and sustain itself. On the other hand, a private and autonomous diffuse power which only acquired political expression when it was co-opted by the State and which entered a trajectory of conflict and defeat when it attempted to articulate itself, even minimally, as an autonomous political force representative of its interests" (93).

If the Empire, he continues, succumbed because of its incapacity to assimilate increasingly organized regional leadership, the oligarchical Old Republic gave way when faced with the onrush of a centralizing State. In this manner, at the moment when local bosses ruled, the State was seen as the property of the group that controlled it. With such utilization of the state apparatus, and with its objectives identified as being the national interest, the creation of a modern State was obstructed, and the perfect configuration of a class society, which occurred late in Brazil, was rendered inviable.

Edgard Carone shows how the crisis initiated in 1929, aggravated in 1937 and during the war, dissolved the productive system based on large rural landholdings. The rural oligarchy had dominated since the colonial period by controlling the means of production, which concentrated on monocultures oriented toward external markets, thus maintaining hegemony and structuring a society to fit its purposes (*A República Liberal*, 133). In general, this situation persists through the colonial period (with the participation of the Portuguese crown), continues through the Empire—when we see a compromise between past and present, resulting in the preservation of an archaic form of power—and into the First Republic, a moment when the oligarchies attain the height of their power. The Revolution of 1930 will represent a moment of crisis in a certain form of articulation in Brazilian society, marking the end of one social group's hegemony (the large landowners), of a mode of relationships between center and periphery, and of an ideological system that had shown signs of exhaustion since the 1920s and whose matrix was elitist liberalism (Fausto, "Nota introdutória," 7–8).

The internal situation is a reflection of the international conjuncture, since Brazil is a peripheral, dependent nation, with a colonial and reflexive economy.[9] And it coincides with the necessity of discovering the country's reality, a sort of sudden awareness of underdevelopment, which appears beginning with the Recife School in the nineteenth century, runs through the work of Euclides da Cunha, and reaches the modernists of 1922 and 1930, besides permeating the work of intellectuals less directly connected to literature, such as the Estado Novo ideologues. This configuration is important since, from the ideological point of view, it traces an arc that goes from around 1880 and extends until the 1950s, with the Instituto Superior de Estudos Brasileiros (ISEB; Higher Institute of Brazilian Studies), totaling some seven decades of formulations about the "Brazilian national character." Such a substratum undeniably underlies and coexists with modernist intellectual production. Consequently, an *archaeology* of Modernism should begin well before 1922, and a more appropriate historicization of Brazilian literature would emphasize the *period of transition* over the aesthetic and stylistic concepts still in vogue.

The eminently ambiguous trajectory I have been examining—and it is worth recalling that the term *transition* carries the notion of contradiction within it, since it refers to what has ceased existing and to what has not yet come into existence—finds one of its high points precisely in the Revolution of 1930, with the end of an exclusively oligarchical State (Ianni, 149).[10] The State then takes command of the process, centralizing economic activity and promoting the country's modernization and capitalization. And the same thing occurs, in a conservative and reactionary fashion, with the implantation of the Estado Novo in 1937. It is important to reiterate that one can perceive the roots of this phenomenon beginning toward the end of the last century, undertaken by ruling elites and sustained ideologically by intellectuals. At the extreme of the trajectory, within the context of the military regime imposed in 1964, we would do well to question the role played by the Escola Superior de Guerra (Higher War College), the National Security Doctrine, and the ideology of IPES (Institute of Research and Social Studies), as fundamental stages in the effective creation of a "modern," authoritarian State. As Edmundo Campos Coelho suggests, both the Estado Novo and 1964 entailed a "project of strengthening the State, implanting authoritarian models of national organization, education, and elite formation" (14).

In light of all of this, I use the category of *transition* with full awareness of the potential problems that it may involve, yet calling attention to the fact that I inscribe a notion of contradiction within it, that is, I conceive of the term ambiguously (thus the italics). In other words, I do not use the concept as if what is being "transformed"—a traditional society—has ceased to exist and what is beginning to appear—a modern society—has been perfectly established.

It is worth repeating that I situate the Brazilian *transition* between 1850 and 1950. The first date marks the year in which slave traffic was finally prohibited, which represented a heavy blow to Brazil's archaic agrarian structure; and, although keeping in mind that it is far from running its course, I limit it to around 1950: with the installation of an automobile industry, Brazil was engaged in import substitution and attending to an expanding internal consumer market. That in itself does not make Brazil a modern country in the complete sense of the word: besides the foreign debt, we all know the price paid for the "economic miracle," and we have seen in the streets the fruit of an unjust distribution of income.

* * *

I will now examine coronelismo with the purpose of illustrating the Brazilian *transition* at the turn of the century—a rural-based society in a process of industrialization and urbanization, with a gradual growth of middle social segments on the political scene and the economic crisis of the then dominant landed sectors.

In her study of the phenomenon, Maria Isaura Pereira de Queiroz stresses that the relationship between the coronel (colonel; landed patriarch, normally with considerable local or regional political power) and his followers is based on the clientelistic mechanism of "favors." In the country's interior, conflicts are more common between families than between those that constitute a family, although they also exist. That is, the coronelistic structure, organized around disputes between those in power and their opposition, is characterized much more by horizontal than by vertical disputes.

In the vertical organization, the colonel is the polarizing and key element (he occupies the center of the system) for determining the individual's place in the social pyramid. As Queiroz explains:

> The question "Who are you?" always and invariably received the same answer: "I'm one of colonel Doe's people." This form of retorting would always give the person asking the necessary coordinates for locating the socio-economic place of the respondent, as well as his political position. The term "people" indicated primarily that it was someone who was not on the same level as the "colonel" or his family; if that were the case, the relationship would be revealed at the beginning to situate the individual within the group (he would say, for example, "I am colonel Doe's cousin"). The use of "people" indicated a person of an inferior level, who may well be a relative, but always a poor one. Secondly, the relationship with colonel Doe allowed the questioner to know immediately if the individual occupied a position supporting or opposed to those in local or regional power, since everyone knew the colonel's position of support or opposition. Finally, colonel Doe's position in relation to other colonels was also well known by all; the individual he protected would espouse the same alliances and enmities in relation to the "people" of other colonels. "Colonel Doe's people" thus meant his dependent clientele. (Queiroz, "O coronelismo numa interpretação sociológica," 156)[11]

The author warns that sociopolitical identification with the colonel was not exclusive to the subaltern classes. Every colonel, in turn, was integrated into a higher stratum, another, more vast group of kindred relations, and the great colonels were authentic, supreme chieftains, frequently transcending local, regional, or state realms and attaining national prominence, as in the case of Pinheiro Machado.

In a vertical reading of the social structure there exists, still according to Queiroz, a tripartite hierarchy involving colonels, campaign workers, and, at the base of political stratification, the electorate. The hierarchy functions, in this sense, regardless of the angle of analysis. If we take the colonel as the center, it is from him that power emanates; if we take a more powerful political chief, on the state level, there will be a hierarchical relationship between him, at the top of the system, and the colonels, along with the respective families and dependents under his control.

Queiroz also points out how the move to the city tended to introduce changes in this scheme, providing a different, and more permanent, profile to the hierarchy.[12] The distribution of houses in villages and small cities founded or protected by local bosses had a common blueprint: in the center the main church, surrounded by the residences of wealthy families and public buildings (contiguity between the ruling landed elites, the Church, and administrative power). Going from this nucleus to the periphery, houses become more modest, with the extremes inhabited by the lowest fractions of the related clientele.

This social and spatial geography, Queiroz notes, goes against that found on large latifundia, where two sectors (one superior, the other inferior) are distributed unevenly in the plantations and fazendas (huge farms) around the mansion. Since in this space the epicenter of power is well defined, the relative interpenetration of distinct social classes does not undo the hierarchy implicit in the structure.

With the advent of villages, the distinctive feature becomes the economic factor. That is, wealth becomes the dividing line of the social organism. Those who possess economic power live with their peers, and, as we move away from this central space, where the most important families in the community live, we find families with fewer possessions and resources. In the urban environment, unlike what occurs on the fazenda, several colonels may coexist. Consequently, the previous identifying element tends to be minimized and relations of power are reestablished on another level, that of the capital of each relative. We are witnessing the emergence of a class society with the adoption of an urban life-style.

In the large, developed cities, the type of personal and affective primary relationship that characterized the colonelistic structure is drastically modified, replaced by a much more complex, impersonal, and indifferent relationship based on categories of individuals (occupational or economic) rather than individuals themselves. Urbanization, demographic expansion, and industrialization, according to Queiroz, ultimately caused the colonelistic system's downfall:

> The populous city, internally differentiated, escapes the colonel's control, which was a very rudimentary kind of authority, to serve a more complex situation. Urban intermediate sectors increase,

> accentuating socio-economic distances between the higher and lower sectors. Little by little, occupational groups are structured which are not only no longer dominated by colonelistic power, but are also opposed to it because of the necessities of the new structures that have arisen. The colonel, who had been the city's "owner," becomes just one element of the power structure, alongside others that may act alternately as his ally or his opposition. ("O coronelismo," 182)

Colonelism, in the final analysis, is the interference of private power in the political domain, rendered possible by the rarefaction of public power and resulting from the superposition of a representative form of government on an inadequate and outdated economic and social organization.[13] A typical phenomenon of the *transition* and an indication and one of the causes of the crisis of rural oligarchies, colonelism results from the commitment of the old order to the strengthening of the State (to which the colonels will adapt and which they will abuse) and can be considered a kind of residual of archaic forms inherited from the Colony, the National Guard, and the Empire as well as, to a great extent, a reflection of the Northeast's isolation halfway between the decline of the plantations and the onset of industrialization (Leal).

Something similar occurs with the cangaço (Northeastern social banditry), equally a sign of the *transition* that requires the services of the sertanejos who became available with the collapse of sugarcane production. The more advanced centers in the south were unable to absorb this inexpensive and unqualified labor force, which provoked, in the 1940s, the beginning of internal migration to large cities, of enormous proportions and disastrous consequences. Colonelism and cangaço, in their final incarnation, could be seen, the political interacting with the economic, as symptoms of a conflict between centralism and localism and as a phenomenon connected to the gradual hypertrophy of the State.

It is precisely when there occur "the abasement of the living conditions of popular sectors" and, with the introduction of paid labor, "the breakdown of customs and values based on traditional relations of domination founded on a network of exchange of services and favors" that Northeastern chapbook literature appears (Terra, 17).

But, of course, hierarchy remained, and authoritarianism was not eliminated from our social formation. Through a peculiar mechanism, surface changes correspond to an underlying lack of change. With the process unleashed by the lieutenants' revolts in the 1920s and the Revolution of 1930, the pendular movement between localism and centralism that pervades Brazilian politics swings to the second pole. During the Vargas dictatorship, authoritarianism and centralism are taken to extremes unprecedented in the nation's history.

Roberto DaMatta has studied the "Brazilian social dilemma" from an anthropological perspective, analyzing diverse cultural rituals (carnival, soccer, "do you know who you are talking to?," the home and the street) in order to underline the fundamentally ambiguous nature of Brazilian society. According to him, Brazil is halfway between a hierarchical society and a fully capitalist egalitarian society (*Carnavais, malandros e heróis*, 191). Fearful of conflict, change, and transformations, Brazilians "have not abandoned the past and yet embrace the future with all of their might" (*A casa e a rua*, 87).

We are thus like the Count of Monte Cristo, a personage who, "at the moment he takes revenge and recovers his honor, reveals himself to be entirely a prisoner of his past" (*Carnavais*, 200). That is, if I understand the symbolism, the Count of Monte Cristo appears on the scene in a violent fashion, but, unlike the abdicator, he does not alter the existing social order but rather enters it and benefits from it. Such a metaphor points toward the paradox of Brazilian modernization and anticipates some of the arguments that will follow. According to DaMatta, "We thus live in an eternal future because we are, in fact, incurably subject to the past. We can only be what we promise ourselves because we are faithful to what we were. Behind the verbal complication, there lies a profound and moving truth: like its heroes, Brazil, the country of the future and of hope, is a society profoundly tied to the past" (*Carnavais*, 201).

Keeping these reflections in mind, let us examine Brazilian Modernism.

* * *

A number of Roberto Schwarz's essays are characterized by an effort to understand Brazilian intellectual life. In a recent study, he writes the following: "The least valued ingredient of our literature is intelligence. Authors are praised because they write well, because they have a memory filled with amusing anecdotes, because they are familiar with remote aspects of the country's life, because they experiment with language, *but not because they have deeply understood the present"* (*Que horas são?* 160–61; emphasis added).

It is within this framework, which was left pending at the end of the previous section, that I plan to dedicate a considerable amount of space to an examination of Modernism, not so much to undertake a circumstantial review of the movement—which, by the way, already comprises an extensive bibliography[14]—but rather to note the shadowy zones that seem to remain obscure because of an interpretation, as Randal Johnson has correctly affirmed, that has privileged the notion of rupture ("Modernism and Authoritarianism in Brazil," 3). Silviano Santiago, in turn, has argued that

> in the 1980s we can finally consider the modernist cycle closed. And we can close it by undertaking a somewhat more unsparing critique than that which has been made until now. "Unsparing," of course, in no way means, in my vocabulary, ill-will toward the movement. But it does mean a certain passionate courage. [. . .] I think the unsparing nature of the reevaluation will be in showing that all modernists were more or less committed to the project of modernizing Brazil, all had a developmentalist mentality, in all the need for being up-to-date was of capital importance, and all wanted to make Brazil enter History, a History that would be pure industrialization. ("Mesa-redonda," 422–23)

Mário de Andrade's famous 1942 lecture (certainly the first thorough evaluation of the movement) already introduced the idea of rupture (235), which, in my view, is accelerated with the reevaluation, in the 1960s, of the work of Oswald de Andrade led by the Concretist poets and appropriated by Tropicalism in popular music. At the extreme of this patrimony of readings and rereadings, the most recent tendency of seeing Modernism as a moment permeated with contradictions is accentuated.

In this range of interpretations, one can further recognize with some clarity three principal lines of analysis: one of rejection, undertaken by those who were attacked by the iconoclastic nature of the movement's heroic phase (I recall, in this regard, Humberto de Campos); second, and fundamentally connected to the expansion of university literature courses, there has prevailed an understanding of Modernism in more independent and favorable terms; and most recently, especially starting with a number of theses and dissertations written at the University of São Paulo, another tendency has arisen, concentrating on the analysis of such modernist documentation as literary reviews (e.g., *Klaxon*) and manifestos.

At the same time, along with the canonical version that understands Modernism as rupture, the opinion has become institutionalized that the movement undertook a survey of Brazilian reality with a less-prejudiced eye (than the romantic vision, for example), capturing a "portrait of Brazil" that revealed an awareness of underdevelopment. Modernism is also frequently discussed in relation to its affinities with European avant-gardes, but not always recognizing the fact that the cultural ground in which the various Old World "-isms" of the first decades of the century flourished was significantly different from that of the incipient metropolis of São Paulo. Finally, another widely disseminated consensus about Modernism concerns dating its eclosion from the Week of Modern Art (February 1922), even when one speaks of "antecedents" or of a premodernism.

More recent studies have addressed the questions involved in Modernism more properly. The works of Francisco Iglésias ("Modernismo: uma reverificação da inteligência nacional") and João Luiz Lafetá (*1930: a crítica e o Modernismo*) call attention to the movement's sociohistorical and ideological substrata: tenentismo, the Prestes column, the decadence of the agrarian "aristocracy," the Revolution of 1930, the creation of the Communist Party and the Center Dom Vital, urbanization, industrialization, greater participation of the middle classes, and the timid appearance of an urban proletariat—all of this intermingled in an "aesthetic project" and an "ideological project" that frequently tended to fuse together. João Alexandre Barbosa's essay, "Linguagem e realidade do Modernismo de 22," alerts us that the revitalization of literary codes undertaken by the modernists responded to the need to renovate language so as to be able to account for the transformations then under way. As a result, Modernism comes to correspond to a moment of transition in Brazilian society (80–81). On another front, Antônio Arnoni Prado (*1922—intinerário de uma falsa vanguarda*) and Silviano Santiago ("Fechado para balanço"), among others, have pointed to the movement's conservative character, for one cannot forget that Integralism also grew out of 1922.

One aspect requiring discussion concerns an *archaeology* of Modernism, that is, its history in terms of discursive practice. The intention of analyzing national reality constitutes a rather old phenomenon among us. It exists in the ambiguous manner in which Gregório de Matos endured colonial status, runs through the eighteenth century of the inconfidentes, is exacerbated with the romantics and their nationalist ideology (Indianism, rural fiction, etc.), continuing with the generation of 1870 gathered around Tobias Barreto and his disciple Sílvio Romero; it finds an exponent in the corrosive interpreter of the Second Reign, Machado de Assis, and is deepened in the diagnoses of such figures as Euclides da Cunha and Lima Barreto. Even among the belle époque's parnassians we find a "portrait of Brazil" engendered by a Francophile elite. It would be naive to think that, to use just one example, the architecture of Rio de Janeiro's Municipal Theater does not represent a specific vision of the country simply because it is a copy of the Parisian Opéra. It would be an error to analyze only the Modernism/nationalism binomial since the concern with understanding Brazilian reality pervades our entire cultural history.

Besides, if the movement does in fact correspond to the process of *transition* in Brazilian society, Modernism's forerunners should be sought where the process begins, around 1850. In the same sense, it would be important to examine more carefully the equivocally denominated premodernism (the term characterizes the 1910s and 1920s in terms of their relationship to Modernism, which is thus privileged as a point of reference). Cities such as Rio de Janeiro and São Paulo already showed indications of modernity with the first electrical transportation, timid signs of a mass culture in advertising, fashion magazines, and billboards. Notions of time and space were being transformed, initiating a climate from which Modernism would certainly benefit (Süssekind, "O figurino e a forja," 33).

It would also be pertinent to outline the modernist intellectuals' ideological position. In São Paulo, they circulated in the salons of a moneyed bourgeoisie that sponsored their trips to Europe; in Rio de Janeiro, the country's capital and administrative center, they were close to the nation's bureaucratic heart and eventually became accomplices of the State as co-opted government employees. Perhaps more important would be to stress that the intelligentsia of the twenties and thirties coexisted with such conservative and authoritarian ideologues as Oliveira Vianna, Azevedo Amaral, Francisco Campos, and Jackson de Figueiredo, and that many modernists participated in the state apparatus during the Estado Novo.[15] In this sense, a *sociology of intellectual life* would be necessary for a full understanding of the period.[16]

* * *

Vargas's mandate during the Provisional Government began with a dispute between old oligarchical groups and the tenentes. Later, it became characterized by the repression of popular movements that included middle- and working-class participants, especially after the failed Communist uprising in 1935. With the decree of the Estado Novo (1937), a good part of the ruling class of oligarchical-bourgeois extraction was in power. Regional oligarchies control state governments; the federal government is composed of agrarian oligarchical groups; the army favors the coup, and the Catholic Church publicly adheres; the productive commercial and industrial classes adulate the new regime; the Integralists help implant the dictatorship and later form part of the "opposition." Excluded are working- and some middle-class parties, a portion of the oligarchical-bourgeois class (especially from São Paulo), and the military and liberals who opposed the Estado Novo (Carone, *O Estado Novo*, 285).

The middle classes had fulfilled an important role since the Old Republic in the sense of forcing a redefinition of the dominant political alliances. Every advancement meant the entrance of dissident groups in restricted circles of power. At the same time, one understands the importance of education—and bacharelismo (rhetorical academic culture)—which differentiated middle segments from the proletariat and provided social validation (Pinheiro, 33, 36).

The extremely centralized Estado Novo intervened in the economy, organizing, administering, and supervising the system of production through consultative organs and agencies. The creation of institutes, such as those of coffee and sugar, "statized" basic agricultural activities, bringing them under the control of the federal government. The Department of the Press and Propaganda (known as DIP) controlled the circulation of information through censorship and sought to mythify the figure of Getúlio Vargas, exploiting the paternalism condensed in the formula "father of the poor." The project of community choirs (canto orfeônico), in which Heitor Villa-Lobos participated, "attempted to make the social body express itself, as long as it did not demand its rights, but rather submitted to the cult of and orders from a leader" (Wisnik, 189). Intellectuals participated in diverse cultural projects, such as the organization of the Service for the National Historical and Artistic Patrimony. Labor legislation (and the creation of the Ministry of Labor) served to placate the working-class demands, which eventually supported Vargas in a period when populism was at its apex. Vargas's history can be summarized as an ability to make alliances, to assimilate or suffocate dissident voices depending on the circumstances of the moment, and increasingly to expand his power, solidifying the corporative Estado Novo.

Marilena Chauí provides us with the ideological framework of the Vargas regime:

> In general terms, from 1920 until 1937 intellectuals were concerned with two major problems which constitute elements for their nationalism: Brazilians' lack of knowledge of Brazilian reality and the need to free themselves from imported political, theoretical and cultural models. On both the left and the right, intellectuals assign themselves the task of creating or awakening a national consciousness, of demonstrating the disjunction between institutions and reality, of producing a scientific and rational policy, and of undertaking a social, political, and cultural *revolution*. The theme of revolution is constant, but its meaning, obviously, is not always the same, depending on the way the "Brazilian crisis" is diagnosed, the way "national salvation" is conceived, and the agents designated to undertake the task. At any rate, one thing is common to all: the presupposition that the understanding and overcoming of the crisis, and revolution itself, depend exclusively on an intellectual elite or a political vanguard. The progressives speak of the need to "civilize Brazil," conservatives of the need to reestablish traditions, order, and the discipline that liberal modernity had destroyed. Both cases,

> however, have one point in common: both "civilization" and tradition demand an organic conception of society and politics, an organicity that depends on the re-creation of the Nation and the installation of a centralized State, even at the expense of having an authoritarian government. (*Inteligência brasileira,* 28–29)

If Chauí's synthesis is correct, it suggests a number of key concepts for an ideological x-ray of the Estado Novo period: elitism, nationalism, centralism, authoritarianism. In fact, such notions appear in the thought of the Brazilian intelligentsia throughout the *transition* from the seignorial era to a more capitalist class society. They are present, for example, in Integralism, with centralized power incarnate in the figure of the National Leader. The green-shirted integralists cultivated God, Fatherland, and Family, fought for National Unity, and preached Order and Authority. Espousing a xenophobic nationalism, personified in the figure of the curupira (a forest spirit with its feet turned backwards, symbolizing a resistance to foreign influences), Integralism disappeared from the scene in 1938, but not without leaving traces in Brazilian authoritarian discourse.

Elitism can be understood as the self-ordained privilege of a group of talented individuals who should hold power and act as a "vanguard," promoting transformations and modernization. It walks hand-in-hand with aryanism/racism and with cultural purism, since elite culture must not be stained by the interference of popular culture. Such elitism, allied with a fascist nationalism and a false erudition, can be detected in Brazil since the belle époque. Mayor Pereira Passos's administration decorated the center of Rio de Janeiro with French-style buildings and statues while it banished the poor to the suburban periphery in a kind of urbanistic version of hierarchy. With the advent of the Republic, the period's intellectuals, in turn, hoped to participate in power (later on they will resign themselves to the political periphery). Judging themselves to be the most apt and capable, crème de la crème, they sought to exorcise all forms of popular culture, in a full-blown "purism" (Sevcenko), an attitude very rooted in the cultural history of Brazil.

The vast majority of intellectuals participated "to a greater or lesser extent in the creation or the dynamization of State apparati, and in this sense they were mouthpieces of the ruling classes' ideologies" (Mota, 287). Ideologue Francisco Campos said, during the Estado Novo, "the worth of a nation is precisely that of its elites"; "transformations did not occur through the action of the primitive mentality of the masses and their leaders, but rather through the influence of the sciences and the arts, philosophers and researchers, scientists, engineers, artists" (Medeiros, 25). Nation and elites become identified with each other, as in the following passage from Azevedo Amaral: "The practice of a democratic regime is only possible where the popular masses spontaneously accept a hierarchy of values and submit without reluctance to the spiritual and political direction of leaders implicitly recognized as guides and orienters of the collectivity" (Medeiros, 53).[17] For him, "power emanates from those who govern, and it cannot therefore, without flagrant absurdity, have its origins attributed to those who are governed" (Medeiros, 103).

If in Azevedo Amaral elitism touches on racism, with state control of eugenics—"stanching the procreative activity of degenerates" (Medeiros, 91)—in Oliveira Vianna this notion is more explicit: "The aryan character of the higher classes, so valiantly preserved in its purity by our ancestors . . . saves us from a lamentable regression. . . . The whole historical evolution of our collective mentality has in effect been nothing but the continuous melioration, through the well-known process of social logic, of ethnically inferior elements of the popular masses toward aryan morality, toward aryan mentality, that is, toward the spirit and character of the white race" (Medeiros, 188–89). In our society, he proceeds, the "higher functions" would pertain "to pure aryans, with the assistance of the superior, aryanized mestizos. They are the ones who, possessing qualities of discipline and education, dominate the uniform and teeming masses of inferior mestizos and, keeping them, through social and juridical compression, within the norms of aryan morality, slowly adapt them more perfectly to the white race's mentality" (Medeiros, 189).[18]

Oliveira Vianna understands the elite as "the most capable," the "best," the "most competent," the "ruling group." He preached government of the "good tyrant"—"a regime of perfect civil freedom without allowing the people to have a minimum of political freedom" (Medeiros, 193). Both the paradox that there is no civil liberty without political freedom and the fact that what is questionable about tyranny is not that it is "good" or "bad," but rather that it is tyrannical, was not an issue.

The authoritarianism of Vianna's thought culminates in the conception of a "powerful national government, dominant, unified, irrevocable," endowed with a hegemonic central power, the State being the agent of the national project. In Brazil, he thinks, "to govern is to overcome disintegrating dispersiveness," strengthening the central power (Medeiros, 168).

Such a set of ideas is crystallized in the Constitution of 1937 (whose primary mentor was Francisco Campos), which instituted the preeminence of the interests of the State above those of the states, municipalities, and individuals, and assured the supremacy of the executive over the other branches. One can thus understand the Estado Novo's Caesarism, defined by Francisco Campos, which situated the president of the Republic as the fulcrum of state organization, to such a point that the State comes to be identified with the President and to be seen as a projection of his will. The head of State becomes synonymous with the nation. Even here one finds the Brazilian *transition:* as formulated by romanticism, the concept of nationalism was one that favored the interests of the agrarian "aristocracy"; now the concept favors those of the State. In other words, the centralization of power supplanted local bossism, with hegemony escaping the control of the landed elites.

This ideological matrix, which revolves around modernization, nationalism, authoritarianism, and populism (added to incorporate, through co-optation, the urban working class) would receive its most finished elaboration, in practical terms, in getulismo (i.e., Getúlio Vargas's ideology) with its strategy of alliances between dissident blocs, with the goal of assimilating them to power and keeping itself in power (Medeiros, 42).

On another front, this matrix will be the object of a more "scientific" treatment in the work of Gilberto Freyre. Starting from the notion of family—used to account for the dominant agrarian system, but which he expands to take in the whole of Brazilian society—Freyre's thought elaborates a "discourse of conciliation" to preserve the pact of 1930.[19] The political weakness of the industrial bourgeoisie, propellant of a project for a new social order, requires the support of traditional sectors, the only ones capable of understanding and preserving the old order (Bastos, 56). In this manner, the *transition* occurs without abrupt changes; the participation of new fractions in power does not exclude the old oligarchical elites, and modernization proceeds, compromised by a large dose of conservatism. Gilberto Freyre "coagulates" the contradictions of the Brazilian social formation, working with oppositions only to empty them of their conflictive nature. His work, seasoned with the exotic spices of his style, ends up providing ideological support to the accord of 1930, guaranteeing the domination of elites and the direction of the bourgeois revolution "from the top down." His perspective is that of the plantation mansion: the analysis of the

> national *ethos* starting from the perception of the *nation as the sum of races,* regions, cultures, and social groups implies eliminating the possibility of a perception of the *social as contradictory,* where domination is repeated precisely because it is exercised over diversity. The role his thought plays permits us to see Gilberto Freyre as an organic intellectual of the pact of 1930 to the extent that his work expresses the possibility of the oligarchies being present in the "new order" then under way, without the necessity for structural changes. (Bastos, 56–57)[20]

One perceives that throughout the period of *transition* and behind a modern-looking façade, certain reactionary constants are present that affect the process of modernization at the base. Traditionalism and authoritarianism are barely disguised.[21] And in this I again find the mythological inclination that avoids questioning the present, which, according to Dante Moreira Leite in reference to the moment after Independence, characterizes a large part of the legacy of the Brazilian intelligentsia (289).

During the Old Republic, intellectuals positioned themselves as a vanguard, drawing up plans (that would benefit them) for the reformation of society—and were marginalized; in the 1930s, ideologues such as Francisco Campos, Azevedo Amaral, Oliveira Vianna, Jackson de Figueiredo (who died in 1928 but whose ideas were influential in the 1930s), Alceu Amoroso Lima, Octávio de Faria, Plínio Salgado, and, somewhat later, Gilberto Freyre—all elaborated a body of thought marked by authoritarianism, elitism, and centralism; from Estado Novo bureaucrat the intellectual will later become the ideologue of developmentalism in the 1950s, when ISEB (Higher Institute of Brazilian Studies) is converted into a "factory of ideologies," to use Caio Navarro de Toledo's expression.

We also now have the elements to question one of the central girders of Brazilian thought in the period of *transition*—the concept of nationalism. The nation is identified with the State and the elites in a scandalous metonymy; nationalism is considered an already defined, given, ideologically impregnated term. A reading of speeches of Vargas's or of ideologues such as Francisco Campos reveal this metonymy to satiation: the Revolution of 1930 was the most positive affirmation of our existence as a "nationality," the coup of 1937 is a manifestation of the "national will," and so forth, continually abstracting the historical dimension, in which the words in quotation marks are never clarified.

Consequently the nation is never seen as *"a political and social practice, a set of actions and relations brought about by discourse and social, political and cultural practices, for which it serves as a reference with several dimensions: empirical (the territory), imaginary (the cultural community and political unity by means of the State), and symbolic (the field of cultural meanings constituted by socio-historical struggles and creations)"* (Chauí, *Conformismo e resistência,* 114).

The nation is not a permanent, immutable concept; it is rethought at every moment, starting from a concrete praxis. Because, still according to Chauí, "cultural beings and objects are not givens, they are *brought about* by certain social and historical practices [. . .]. For something to be *this or that* and *this and that* it is necessary for it to be brought about or constituted by social practices" (122).

Instead of discourses that problematize the nation, we have discourses for the nation, in the nation's name, which claim to be absolute and atemporal truths, unrelated to the practices that generated them. An analysis of the ideology of Brazilian intellectuals from the Old Republic until the 1950s, notably in their manipulation of notions such as "Brazilian culture" or "nationalism," reveals how tensions resulting from the establishment of a class society are obfuscated and how much the whole debate about dependency is camouflaged (Mota, 269).[22]

* * *

I will now turn toward Brazilian Modernism, especially the literary production of the 1930s, with the intellectual atmosphere that effervesced during the period as a background. I believe, for example, that we can now analyze with more propriety the movement's vision of Brazil. In its initial moments it transmitted, as Alfredo Bosi has suggested, either a harlequin São Paulo, the "space of modernity," or a mythical territory, a Brazil from the roots, of a radical primitivism (*Céu, inferno,* 118). The international cult of modernity appears mixed with the practice of Brazilian traditions, with the search for the past, the colonial artistic legacy (the modernist's famous trip to Minas Gerais), the indigenous heritage. And in 1930, when one might expect the problematization of the contradictions of Brazilian society by way of a more political literature, fiction takes on a tone of nostalgia of the past, through the pen of the "chroniclers of the murdered house," descendants of the great patriarchal families who attempt to restore the seignorial scene in the space of literary representation. In sum, one must keep in mind that Modernism offers the apprehension of a given social group about Brazil, an apprehension permeated by this same group's historical and class position. That is, in the final analysis, the same social class that accepts the pact of 1930. At the very least it is curious that there is little corrosive questioning of the present in the production left by Modernism, with a corollary absence of historicity, precisely at a moment when everyone seemed to be involved in the task of modernizing the country.

What leaps before one's eyes is that Modernism projects into the future that which it attempted to rescue from the past (Ronaldo Brito, 15), in a paradoxical conception of modernity, making the central notion of modernization, implicit in the entire modernist project, suffer from the same contradictory character. As Florestan Fernandes emphasizes, with great propriety, Brazilian modernization does not appear as a natural result of the internal evolution of modern capitalism; rather, it takes shape as a political crisis of the old colonial system (*A revolução burguesa no Brasil,* 7).

One thus concludes, first, that it is a mistake to see Modernism exclusively as rupture. If it is correct to say that it arises against the verbose and pretentious rhetoric practiced by the Parnassians, it is also necessary, on the other hand, to variegate rupture and reexamine the extent to which Modernism represents continuity in relation to previous moments of Brazilian cultural discourse, particularly romanticism, which everything seems to indicate that Modernism recasts and deepens. Manuel Bandeira already pointed in this direction (Guimarães, 59), and essayists have focused, more recently, on how Modernism ends up systematizing diverse ideas, elaborating them in a more organic fashion.

Second, one confirms how it is insufficient to use just one term to account for such disparate aesthetic and ideological projects as those of Oswald de Andrade and Plínio Salgado, to restrict myself to an extreme case. There are modernisms and modernisms. In a more stylistic sense, José Guilherme Merquior attempted to separate the wheat from the chaff in a study titled "A estética do Modernismo do ponto de vista da História da Cultura," distinguishing between the moderns in Modernism and the nonmoderns who are also usually included in the movement.

It would be prudent to reserve the term *Modernism* to refer to the movement that started with the Week of Modern Art in 1922. Nevertheless, it is truly imperative to change the usual tactic of historicization, tied to "period styles," of the Brazilian literary corpus. I have already alluded to the contradictions of Brazilian modernization, which seems to me to render Modernism itself problematic. Taking the movement without reservations, we should not forget that within it circulated the discourse that leads to the Estado Novo.

More relevant for my reasoning, however, would be to bring into the debate the concept of *modernity* (understood as a plural conception of the discourse) and see if it is appropriate to the modernist project. I do not intend to explore this topic in excessive detail, since I am more interested in placing canonical versions of Modernism in check. I will thus undertake a brief digression on the *Quijote* before ending with a rapid discussion of Modernism's modernity.

* * *

It would be difficult, in the age of the nuclear threat, to imagine the impact that discoveries such as those of Galileo Galilei, Harvey, and Kepler had in the medieval edifice. In that ordered, limited world of restricted, finite, and static dimensions, hierarchically structured both in celestial and sociocultural realms, they inspired the notion of the infinite, of perpetual motion, of relativity, inaugurating a modern conception of the universe. Allied with the feudal nobility, the Church's dogmatic control was inevitably affected. Discoveries in the field of science would transform ecclesiastic teachings, which made use of and manipulated Aristotle to explain the cosmos: "When Father Scheiner confessed his discovery of Sun spots to his superior, the latter, who refused to believe, was to have said: 'I have read Aristotle many times from beginning to end, and I can assure you that I found nothing similar in him. Go, my son, be tranquil and certain that what you see as Sun spots are defects of your lenses or your eyes'" (Mousnier, 226).

The Church was also losing ground on the cultural front, with the humanists, the secularization of teaching, and the creation of universities, and in the political and economic fields, with the gradual appearance of the bourgeoisie and the formation of strong national states, supported by the new class. There were also the more properly religious aspects: the breaks from Catholicism of the Greek Orthodox Church and then of the Protestant Reformation.

It is not by chance that the period's art (sixteenth and seventeenth centuries, Mannerism and Baroque) is marked by this tension and these contradictions: dilacerated between the material and the spiritual, the earthly and the heavenly, the mundane and the divine, faith and reason, European man could not help but transfer to the artistic field the profound crisis civilization was going through. Capitalism and modern science were born, but medieval culture, impregnated with religiosity and mysticism, was still present, even after the tremors of Renaissance humanism, creating obstacles to the protagonists of the new epoch to become totally familiar with it.

This horizon seems important for understanding not only works of the seventeenth century, but also for discerning the emergence of modernity itself. In play was a confrontation of versions: the version of the Church against the version of the Copernicans; the Catholic version against the Protestant version; the bourgeois version against that of the nobility or the Church. These conflicts brought with them the question of power. To illustrate: the Church was not interested in the translation of the Bible to Romance languages, since, by reading the Bible in his or her own language, each believer could interpret it in his or her own manner, thus escaping from official ecclesiastical control. One of the decisions of the Council of Trent prohibited the free interpretation of the Bible, which should be read in consonance with the Church's teaching. Religious disputes could not disguise their political content.

In the Spanish case the situation tended to be aggravated. Spain clearly set its feet in tradition, taking sides with the world that was in crisis. It was not only the bulwark of Catholicism and the ardent defender of the Counter-Reformation, but it also dreamed of the reconstruction of the Roman Empire under Carlos V (living desengaño [desillusion] still in the Habsburg dynasty), a pretension in which are perceptible notorious ambitions of unity, totality, and universality: Catholic unity and a universal monarchy were the proud Hispanic ideals of the sixteenth century, in contrast with the rest of Europe, where, enriched by Renaissance individualism, national states were formed and religious fragmentation prevailed.

The death of God dates from the dawning of the modern age. Recalling the conflict between medieval theocentrism and the anthropocentrism of the humanists, God can be understood here as an Ur-code that overdetermines all meanings in the context of the Middle Ages, a code manipulated by the clergy and the aristocracy, thus impeding the circulation of meanings within Western culture. With its decline, the interpretive game is freed and modernity begins. In discursive terms, modernity arises in the West when truth is decentered and opened to the vertiginous abyss of interpretation, giving way to the collision of different versions.

In this sense, *Don Quijote* is a novel of extreme modernity, as Foucault notes in *Les mots et les choses*. Instead of a transparent world, in which there exists a contiguity between sign/language/representation and referents, with signifieds given beforehand by God, the *Quijote* reveals the fissure between language and the world. The knight of La Mancha searches for the meaning of the reality around him, starting with the references obtained from his reading of chivalry novels, but he finds no similarity. Something has definitively been broken. He must give sense to the world. In this line of reasoning, the obsessive rationalism of the eighteenth century could be seen as a vain effort to grasp the ultimate laws that rule the universe, signaling this fracture and lack of contiguity.

In the *Quijote* versions collide—from the conflicting versions of the protagonist and his squire Sancho Panza, to a discussion of truth (which is decentered in the novel) and fiction. In summary, as Milan Kundera writes: "When God slowly abandoned the place from where he had directed the universe and its order of values, from where he had separated the Good from the Bad and had given meaning to each thing, Don Quijote left his house and was no longer in a condition to recognize the world. In the absence of a supreme judge, a terrible ambiguity suddenly arose; the only truth was decomposed into hundreds of relative truths that men share among themselves" (13).

The discovering of the symbolic and thinkers such as Darwin, Marx, Freud, Einstein, and Saussure will complete this decentering of man and truth, and the human sciences will end up revealing how the subject is in fact fragmented, how reality depends on language, and how meaning is always in dissemination.

* * *

A series of problems arises when we transpose this problematic to the Brazilian cultural context. From the outset, keeping what was just outlined in mind, what Western culture experienced as a crisis of meaning, starting from approximately the end of the sixteenth century, would occur in Brazil only around the turn of the century, exacerbated in 1930—a fact which incites numerous reflections. One of the crucial distinctions would be that in the Brazilian case (although in the European context the question of the social group is no less relevant) it is clear that what is questioned is the monopoly of a social segment, that of the agrarian patriarchy. Another, to avoid excessively prolonging the discussion, would be that which suggests the collapse of authoritarian discourse in the West and the preservation of authoritarianism in Brazil, since, according to what I affirmed above, Brazilian cultural discourse, even considering potential fissures, is far from being qualified as *plural,* and this is, in my opinion, the great debate to be engaged in various levels of Brazilian social life—the search for a pluralization that makes possible the emergence of *difference* in a traditionally authoritarian society.

I will thus merely outline the problem: can we find such a conception of modernity in all of the literature generated by Modernism? Can we see in its fictional production a discourse that avoids hierarchies, that puts meaning in circulation and kindles interpretive play? Or, even more important, do we find an abyssal *problematization of language* which, since language is crucial for social interaction and change, ends up by historicizing all discourse? Are we faced with an effectively transgressive literature?

As I will emphasize ahead, there is an *absence of History* (and I have in mind a textual inscription) in the Brazilian literature created around the 1930s. In the past century, literary texts were by and large produced by writers who belonged, or aspired to belong, to dominant, agrarian sectors; they were read basically by these same groups; and they developed themes concerning this same hegemonic sector (or they viewed peripheral segments from the perspective of the landed "aristocracy"). It is for this reason that one can say that nineteenth-century literature is a self-portrait of the ruling fractions linked to exports which reduplicated the society that produced it. If this interpretation is correct, it would be unfounded to think of such fiction as transgressive. Forced to share power with the new industrial sectors at the turn of the century, during the *transition* these oligarchies faced a historical vacuum, losing their raison d'être (since they are not the only agents of the process anymore), which will lead them to forge alliances in 1930. The lack of historicity, as a discursive feature, in the period's literature is not only homologous with reality, but it also translates the useless effort to bring back, in the space of literary production, the past. Here, again, it is equally ungrounded to speak of *transgression*.

Informed about aesthetic achievements and the desire to reconcile a new and up-to-date form of expression, borrowing from the European avant-garde, with a submersion in the country's reality, we have said that Modernism corresponds to a moment of *transition* in Brazil, from an agrarian society to an urban-industrial one. The renovation of language was indispensable, since the literary codes in vogue in so-called premodernism could no longer account for the cultural complexity that it sought to express. One must consider further that there also occurred a professionalization of the writer and an expansion of the publishing industry, with the consequent broadening of the reading public and a proliferation of cultural goods, obvious when we think of the boom of mass media like the radio. This perhaps explains, at least in part and indirectly, the nonexperimental tendency of the period's texts (far different from the radicality of Oswald de Andrade's *Memórias sentimentais de João Miramar* and *Serafim Ponte-Grande* or Mário de Andrade's *Macunaíma*), perhaps destined to satisfy the demands of the growing urban middle sectors.

The primitivist component in certain manifestations of the "heroic phase" will be responsible for the mythification of Brazilian culture, leaving the questioning of the truly contradictory Brazil to the 1930s and a more political literature. Even this opinion, espoused by Alfredo Bosi ("As letras na Primeira República," 315–16), needs to be shaded, since there exists a considerable mythification (of the *seignorial scene*) also in the novelistic heritage of the second modernist moment, detectable even in the novels that sought to be attentive to the country's urban scenario. Such a literature is turned more to the past than the present, more inclined toward the mythical than traversed by History. The examination of various texts linked to the Brazilian *transition*, by different authors, reveals, fundamentally, that in them is narrated the very same story—that of the decline of the patriarchal elites. Because this fiction lived the contradictions of the *transition* and shared the ideological climate discussed above.

Another possible breach would be to question to what extent the movement truly took advantage of elements deriving from popular manifestations, and, in this case, to what point did it develop a truly national matrix. A study by José Miguel Wisnik shows that, at least in relation to modernism's musical nationalism, emerging popular culture was rejected (for example, that of urban blacks, which revealed social contradictions in the urban space), since it disorganized the centralized, homogeneous, and paternalistic vision of official culture, which passed for "national." In its place, sources of rural popular culture were stylized and idealized (133). Could there not be an identical paternalism, in relation to folklore and the popular imaginary, in many of Modernism's texts that incorporate legends and myths? It is useful, in this regard, to recall the deeply rooted tradition of cultural initiatives undertaken by intellectuals sheltered under the protective wings of the state bureaucratic apparatus, as if only the State made History, as if cultural producers were only historical to the extent that they participate in the State or in a project of the State (Novaes, 9).

In sum, I have a certain difficulty in finding, within Modernism, a conjugation of *modernity* (in the sense outlined above), a *questioning of language,* and a *historicization of discourse.* The names that occur to me, rather dissonant when we think of the two initial instants of the movement, are Oswald de Andrade and Graciliano Ramos—and it would be interesting to analyze them from this perspective.[23]

I think that such topics will achieve a better profile in Brazilian literature in the 1940s, in the work of Guimarães Rosa and Clarice Lispector, in which we can unveil a radical shredding of language, exploring it from the inside out and permitting History (although such texts do not allude to it in documentary terms) to traverse, in the very folds of the narrative fabric, novels such as *Grande sertão: veredas* or *A paixão segundo GH.* In reference to the latter, by Clarice Lispector, although it is a text that seems to be alienated from History, it is a viscerally modern narrative. And Guimarães Rosa, beyond the alchemy to which he submits the verb, opening it to History, brings to modernity an archaic universe, rewritten in an acutely contemporary key. Signification circulates in this novel, where everything is movement and ambiguity and where the existential problematic of modern mankind is transplanted to the sertão of Minas Gerais. Through his narration, Riobaldo searches for the meaning of his errant passage.

It would seem to be opportune, in this context, to ask to what point these two narrators in fact violate the dominant authoritarian norm in Brazilian letters or to what extent they are its heirs. If, on the one hand, one can write that the fact that Riobaldo is allowed to narrate signifies a change (he is not an educated narrator who appropriates the speech of the other, as had occurred in Alencar and so many regionalists), on the other hand, analyses such as that of Consuelo Albergaria show "the author as an instance of power" in Rosa.[24] And, furthermore, one might see the whole of Rosa's monumental fresco as a requiem for a rural Brazil, massacred by the voracious steamroller of progress. In effect, History withdraws into the protagonist-narrator, internalized in the subject. Riobaldo's "human 'sertão'" prevails, while the geographical and social sertão disappears after the ex-gunman's story is reconstituted. With this, its transgressive strength is undone, and Riobaldo himself becomes a landowner on the banks of the São Francisco River and becomes pure memory, engaged in contemplation and accommodated in his creaking hammock.

In Clarice Lispector's case the question assumes a feminist contour: is there a feminist discourse in her fiction? In *Uma aprendizagem* it is the masculine character Ulisses who makes it possible for Lóri to find her identity. If the assertion is correct, we would continue under the primacy of a masculine and patriarchal order, which reigns in Brazilian fiction, alongside its authoritarian model.

Despite the avant-garde experimentalism of the 1920s or proposals such as antropofagia, perhaps only in the mid-1940s, with Lispector and Rosa, does Brazilian literature enter an authentic *modernity.* Curiously, and not by mere chance, from the same period are more incisive reflections about the country's reality (Caio Prado, Jr., Florestan Fernandes in relation to blacks, and Roberto Cardoso de Oliveira concerning Indians, to mention just a few names).

If one of the central characteristics of Western cultural discourse, announced, for example, in works such as the *Quijote,* is a plurality of versions inscribed in the discursive fabric, with the decentering of truth and an opening toward the play of signification, then modern discourse is *plural* and in it *meaning is displaced.* In the fiction of the 1930s, in a general sense, I do not see such *modernity.* The period's literary production is centered by the perspective of the declining seignorial class, repeating the patriarchal and masculine vision that seems to traverse a significant part of Brazilian literature. The historical crisis, as a hegemonic group, of that social segment at that moment leads the novel to restore the *seignorial scene* on the level of literary representation, normally mythifying the good old days of the coronéis. As if immune to the present, this fictional production in truth laments the decline of the rural world which weighs on the Brazilian social and cultural tradition and which was in some sense being questioned in the 1930s. The period's most acute contradiction resides precisely in this: in a historical moment that demanded major transformations, political options, and the definition of a new direction, literature, as well as a good part of intellectual production, acquires a nostalgic contour and turns its back on the present and on History. Or, as in the case of the initial works by Jorge Amado, it teleologically catapults History to a future without a class society.

Such a centering, moreover, impedes the appearance of other voices and creates this discomfort of historical absence, with history understood as interaction and effective exchange between individuals: social relations between characters are hierarchical, based on submission and patronage, residuals of slavery. Furthermore, it is a literature written by members of this social segment, about this social segment, or, when it speaks of the other, it does so from a seignorial perspective; since this segment was turned toward the reconstitution of the past, toward its symbolic reconstruction, which led to mythification, history has no place in such texts, since it was beyond the very project of these dominant sectors, which were confronting an industrial and urban bourgeoisie in full ascension. If the assertion is pertinent, one would have to separate modernists from moderns and emphasize the conservative and authoritarian character of the country's modernization.

Modernity is truly installed in Brazilian fiction starting with the moment when there exists a radical *problematization of language.* Language is a symbolic process that facilitates socialization among individuals and it is thus permeable to History. The historicization of Brazilian literature needs to be revised—it is necessary not only to rethink the whole process of the canonization of authors and works or the aesthetic-stylistic criteria which have until now been privileged. It is also necessary to find *discursive categories* that anchor approaches to texts. This would invert chronological periodization, which betrays an evolutionary and positivist conception of temporal process, and take us back to the second half of the nineteenth century, if we wished to locate our first abyssally modern writer: Machado de Assis—who excavated the corners of language, denounced hypocritical masks, and made faces with the sharp stiletto of modernity.

Second Strand: The Beads

The Self-Portrait and the Back of the Portrait

In this chapter I examine one central tendency of the nineteenth-century Brazilian novel and then contrast it with the incomparable work of Machado de Assis in order to show how much Machado stands out from the norm. I will concentrate primarily on José de Alencar, taken here as a paradigmatic nineteenth-century Brazilian novelist.

Alencar's novels betray a closed worldview corresponding to a hegemonic agrarian society, while the dialogical nature of Machado's narrative unveils the *transition,* a fracture introduced into the monolithic and authoritarian edifices erected since the dawn of the Colony and the national period by the landed or seignorial "aristocracy."

It is well known that Alencar attempted to compose a vast mural of Brazil, publishing urban, Indianist, rural, and historical novels, a sort of tropical "human comedy" sketching a portrait of the nation. Alencar can be discussed in relation to our literature's emancipation, which corresponded to the political task undertaken during the Second Reign (1840–1889). Writers such as Alencar sought to give their literature a national, specifically Brazilian character, freeing it particularly from Portugal's traditions of the former metropolis. Such a project matched romantic local color and nationalism perfectly, both of which walked hand in hand with the idealization so common in the period's letters.

In Europe, romanticism can be understood, schematically, as an aesthetic and cultural answer to such events as the French and Industrial Revolutions. In opposition to materialist pragmatism, which had gradually begun to rule in an increasingly competitive society dominated by exchange value, and to the progressive reflux of religious experience, the romantic poet counterposed the super-valorized individual, attributing to him the capacity for reintegration in the whole. The romantic writer is afflicted by a malaise in bourgeois civilization, whose gray existence lacks heroic adventures and authentic values. This frequently gives romantic art a countercultural matrix.

In Brazil, however, the panorama was different. Independence not only left the Ancien Régime intact, based on a dependent, slaveholding, agrarian, export economy, but was also unable to stimulate full industrialization. Besides, the romantic artist was coopted by the monarchical State, with the goal of placing the country alongside civilized nations and thus serving the cause of national affirmation expressed by Dom Pedro II.

It was not by chance that the emperor supported Indianism, in a clear recognition of its ideological function (I am thinking, for example, of his actions as a Maecenas of the group which published the review *Niterói* and of his support of the publication of the poem "Confederação dos Tamoios," by Gonçalves de Magalhães, whom the monarch honored and made an instrument of his cultural policy). The Indian was brave and loyal, assuring the elites a glorious genealogy for their nobility. He was ethnically pure, thus freeing these same elites from the shame of mixed blood. He was idealized as if a gentleman with a cudgel.

Alencar wrote an Indianist trilogy where idealization is flagrant. Suffice to see how he transposes the Victorian moralism of his own social group to the Tupi woman, in one of the notes to *Ubirajara* (150–51). Equally idealized is the figure of the sertanejo (backlander), who is also characterized as specifically Brazilian, when the rural, sertanista novel succeeds the exhausted Indianist vein.

I want to emphasize that if, as I suppose, the idea of portraying Brazil (and its genesis) by using and idealizing the Indian or backlander as a national symbol was part of Alencar's purpose, then in this we can discover a compromising displacement. From the outset I should stress that I am not demanding a narrow "realism" from Alencar. Rather, I hope to detect in his literary project a sleight of hand that seems to be one of the fundamental characteristics of Brazil in the nineteenth century. According to Nestor Goulart Filho, a scholar of the period's architecture, house interiors were often covered with paintings or decorative wallpaper reproducing Greco-Roman motifs or suggesting a distant landscape radically different from the reality outside the door, with its shanties and slaves (Schwarz, *Ao vencedor as batatas*, 20).

The idea of being "misplaced," to recall the words of Roberto Schwarz, seems to rule the cultural life of the times. Brazilians imported romanticism and liberalism, which were climatized to the provincial and nonindustrial milieu of an economy based on slave labor. In this context, liberal ideas were, so to speak, excrescent.

Brazilian social reality thus enters Alencar's work on the sly. It is not to be found on the surface of his narratives but rather in the background that the surface covers up. Taking *Til* as a brief illustration, one observes that the first level of the plot places us before a quartet of adolescents engaged in innocent flirting and coquetry. In the background of this novel of manners parade the three large social segments left by colonization: landowners, "free men," and slaves.

To the extent that the "free men," in the final analysis dependent on the landowners, existed under the protective wings of the dominant group, Brazilian social stratification tended toward polarization: landowners on the top (free men aligned with them) and slaves at the bottom. The existent intermediate gradation continued being overdetermined by the hierarchy. We could draw such a social structure as being composed of a series of concentric circles. In the middle, sovereign and all-powerful, is the landowner who accumulates the roles of father (because it is a patriarchal society) and male (because its is a society based on the male figure). The closer to the center of power, the greater the social prestige; the farther away, the greater the social inferiority. To exemplify, the firstborn son enjoys the privileges of the future heir of paternal wealth. At the other extreme, the field slaves are treated like animals. Starting with the figure who occupies the center, the remaining places on the social scale are determined by way of hierarchical relations of power, that is, from dominant to dominated. The hierarchy persists even if we don't consider the landowner's position: domestic slaves had primacy over those who sweat in the fields. Being a slave, in short, was a stigma to be avoided at all costs. Manual work, because it was identified with servitude, was seen (and is so until today) as vile and unworthy. Many freed slaves bought slaves, so as to be treated as masters.

Historians of nineteenth-century Brazil are unanimous in affirming that what stands out in the period is the existence of slavery. The black African was, consequently, much more present in the daily life of the nineteenth century than was the Indian, who, when not ravaged by illness or violence, took refuge in the depths of the forest. It is therefore understandable that choosing the slave as a central figure of the novel during the period would be to discuss the very foundations of the slaveholding society. For this reason, when he appears in nineteenth-century fiction, the black normally appears whitened, as in the case of the slave Isaura, in the eponymous novel by Bernardo Guimarães, to mention only one title. In consonance with this tendency of avoiding the theme of slavery, such corollary themes as labor and violence, which were also important in the relations of economic and social production, were equally discarded.

But the slave problem was too urgent to disappear, and it entered Alencar's narrative indirectly, through the back door. The protagonist of *Senhora,* Aurélia, says the following: "What you call slavery is no more than the violence that the strong exercise against the weak [. . .]. I know of only one tyrant who makes real slaves, and that tyrant is love" (159). Again the displacement: the true question (slavery as a form of violence imposed on the weak by the strong) shifts to the level of "tyrant love," impeding any real discussion of slavery as violence. Said in another way: the master-slave relation—a hierarchical relation of power and domination—which is so apparent in social reality, appears unfocused and transposed to the amorous sphere in Alencar's text.

Many couples serve as protagonists in José de Alencar's plots. Amorous relations are treated in terms of "master and slave." Remembering that being a slave is a stigma indicating social inferiority, examples of "tyrant love" include the following: in *Lucíola,* the courtesan Lúcia is the "slave," Paulo, the student who is a candidate for high society gentleman, the "master"; in *Iracema,* the "slave" is the virgin Tabajara Indian girl and the "master" is the white Portuguese warrior, Martim; in *O guarani* the Goitacás Indian Peri is the "slave," and the blond Cecília, daughter of the feudal lord D. Antônio de Mariz, is the "mistress"; in *O sertanejo,* the "slave" is the cowherd Arnaldo, the "mistress" is Dona Flor, the landowner's daughter. Blacks are represented only secondarily in

Alencar's prose. Seen as "slaves" of love are, respectively, the woman, the Indian (male or female), and the backlander. These personages, significantly, are depicted as heroes, praised by their narrators in an attempt to forge a national mythology, molding the "Brazilian man."

The master-slave relationship, scandalous on the social plane, is captured asymmetrically by literary texts and transferred to sentimental intrigues. The novels speak of the "servitude" of love, omitting the dominant's tyranny over the dominated in a slave society. To be a "slave" of love, with captivity representing a scar that socially represses those who endure it, includes diverse categories, such as to be a woman, to be an Indian, and to be a backlander. In the latter two cases, I should stress, Alencar's text attempted to outline a national identity by choosing the Indian and the cowherd as prototypes of Brazilianness. To exalt them as heroes is, again, a masking displacement concealing their inferiority, reaffirmed quietly in the text's background.

If this assertion is correct, it undercuts the oft-praised nationalism of Brazilian romantic fiction, sung to the four winds by certain critics, because the concept of the nation at stake is, in fact, the one that interested and suited the ruling landed elite, which intended both to sculpt its own cultural profile and to proclaim its political supremacy. Novelists (normally members of the seignorial class or those aspiring to become members) created these heroes and betrayed themselves in so doing, since the characters ultimately have no voice. The characters who supposedly represent Brazilian cultural specificity are called forth only to be, paradoxically, stifled by the values of the dominant, patriarchal elites, because, in reality, these narratives deify the white male and the landowner (that is, those effectively in power during the Second Reign), never the Indian, the backlander, or the woman. Even when, as in the case of Alencar, they apparently seek to understand the other, who belongs to the social minority, Indianist and rural texts, and even works such as *Lucíola,* discard such figures, since they were created with the prejudiced vision of the seignorial class and understood in terms of the ruling elite's values. The novels never attempted to adopt the perspective of the other and thus establish an alterity, as modern anthropology might recommend.

Consequently, any indication of character movement from the

periphery toward the center of power is rejected. In *O sertanejo,* Dona Flor, the landowner's daughter, says to the cowherd Arnaldo, who had touched her: "Don't forget your place," "I am not your equal" (143). What one observes, in conclusion, is that the nineteenth-century novel provides a self-portrait of the society that wrote and read it, reproducing, in literary representation, the hierarchical barriers that characterized social reality. It did not generate any form of transgression. Even when it attempts to deal with the other, it ultimately returns, despite itself, to the image of the ruling sectors, at least to the extent that the seignorial point of view presides over the narrative background.

Although I have limited my analysis to Alencar, I believe I can include in a single gesture of reading most characters of the Brazilian novel of the last century: the relations between them are markedly hierarchical, with the landed elites (the seignorial class), the male (the masculine order), and the father (the patriarchal order) occupying the dominant position. The discourse thus created—and this is of central interest to the current analysis—is authoritarian in that it does not go beyond meanings suited to the consolidation of the landed oligarchies' hegemony. In other words, meanings that express other sectors of society generally do not circulate in the nineteenth-century Brazilian novel. From this perspective one can understand how Alencar's closed novelistic production corresponded to an equally closed society, which eventually uses novelistic representation, almost despite itself, to look at itself in the mirror. The dissonance that breaks through this "narrow circle" dominating Brazilian prose narrative arises only with the work of Machado de Assis.

* * *

The difference between Machado de Assis and other nineteenth-century Brazilian writers begins with their respective biographical trajectories. Other writers were by and large from landowning fractions of the dominant class or willing to be part of it. Alencar was a senator of the Empire and, despite his literary Indianism, as such he did little for the indigenous nations. Moreover, he was a fervent proslavery advocate. Machado, in contrast, rose above his class. Of humble origin, he ascended socially, was accepted by higher classes, and occupied a privileged yet displaced position: he no longer belonged to the less-favored sectors, but he could not totally identify with the "aristocracy" that accepted and venerated him. This contradictory situation provided him with a caustic critical perspective from which to scorn the new, moneyed bourgeoisie. Machado, furthermore, seems to occupy an ambiguous position. He regrets the nouveaux riches' lack of good manners, finesse, and culture, which somehow makes him a traditionalist. This traditionalism is detectable, for example, in his discretionary conduct as president of the Brazilian Academy of Letters. At the same time, his provocative writing develops a narrative texture without precedence in Brazilian literature. This section of the chapter will briefly examine some of Machado's more relevant innovations on the level of novelistic composition.

Alencar's plots involve cause-and-effect relationships, and, despite some easily identifiable, temporal cuts, they are structured according to a linear and chronological sequence of events. In general, the narrator is omniscient, and he demiurgically manipulates his fictitious personages who succumb to manichaeism—the heroes have only good qualities, the villains only defects—and who are psychologically shallow. Alencar's text, furthermore, tends toward a univocality of meaning that renders difficult a plurality of interpretations. Symptomatic of this authoritarian control of meaning are the prefaces, notes, and afterwords, in which the author, like a zealous father, predetermines the possibilities of reading his work. With respect to foreign literature, the attitude of Alencar's prose is one of reverence, seeking legitimacy. To confer the status of cultural fact on the sertão, the raw material used to compose *O sertanejo,* the narrator must compare the main character to the heroes of European literature and Greco-Roman mythology. Only thus would the period's readers (notably women and students living in a predominantly urban environment who are familiar with this tradition and generally unfamiliar with the far-off reaches of the country) recognize his value.

Machado's writing challenged all of the narrative standards crystallized in Alencar's exemplary production. Instead of following the models of the French novel, as was the fashion at the time, Machado drank from the waters of eighteenth-century British fiction, particularly Laurence Sterne's *Tristram Shandy.* His plots are not structured in terms of causality, but rather are diluted and fluid. Consequently, the characters and, especially, the commentaries the narrator weaves about the narrated events and the actions of his fictional personages are in the forefront. Machado intertwines the narrative as such with digressions and meditations of diverse natures, without respecting a strict chronology, which is substituted by an incessant forward and backward movement in time. Deepening his characters' psychology to the point of revealing their most intimate motivations, human weaknesses and vanities, showing the necessity of social masks, Machado confers on his dramatis personae an extremely ambiguous, paradoxical, and non-manichaean profile.

Besides this, Machado's narrator is surprisingly modern. He is no longer a central structuring voice commanding the narrative from above. To the contrary, the narrator activates discrepant voices, without establishing precedence among them, questioning even his own version of the facts he relates. The truth of the texts is transformed into a question of point of view, and, as such, it is overdetermined by interests in play.

I find two aspects of capital importance in Machado's writing. First, Machado incribes his work under the primacy of relativization—and in this he inserts himself into the core of modernity. Problematizing absolute truths, Machado's text is notable for polyphony, for conflict between versions, for the relativism of values and meanings, for the moral ambiguity of his characters. Consequently, and contradicting the main lines of the Brazilian novel as discussed above, Machado undercuts hierarchies. His narrator does not adopt the point of view of the dominated, who are practically absent from his work. Yet, hovering over, but simultaneously moving within the heart of the upper classes, and armed with humor and irony, Machado's narrator is able to capture, from within, the contradictions of the members of the dominant fractions, dismantling the notion of hierarchy to the extent that he places power in check and reveals how meaning depends on who is in power.

Second, and still as a function of the fundamentally dialogical nature of his fiction, Machado establishes, through citations and allusions to other texts (literary, philosophical, or even discourses of various origins, ranging from the Bible to cookbooks), an intertextual dialogue that semantically directs his writing, in a double (at least) textual orientation. This relationship with other texts, normally from the European literary tradition, does not occur, as in Alencar, in the molds of a reduplication. Its most important characteristic is parody. The appropriation of other discourses, literary or not, always passes through a parodical sieve, reorienting its meaning and transforming the text-matrix into a typically Machadian diction. The narrator dialogues with the narrative, with the characters, with the reader (the implied reader), with other texts and discursive models. Machado explores the level of enunciation, bringing the dialogical nature of his writing inside novelistic composition itself. When I recall that parody, a redimensioned assimilation of another text, will reemerge in a writer like Oswald de Andrade during Modernism, I ask if Machado was not anthropophagous avant la lettre.

Language is also affected. Behind a style which at first glance seems chaste, Machado overturns common sense, undermines clichés, takes apart stuffed and pompous rhetoric based on catchy phrases, and satirizes false erudition. The critique of all these verbal practices occurs within language itself, in the folds of which Machado's narrator denounces the sclerosis of aphorisms and cultural ostentation derived from the Brazilian intelligentsia's academic formation.

Perhaps one of Machado's texts which clearly reveals the principles that I have synthesized, notably that of relativization, is "O alienista" ("The Psychiatrist," in English translation), the first novella of his so-called mature phase, published in the volume *Papéis avulsos* (1882). It is a story with an allegorical nature, at least in that it constitutes an acute reflection on power (and the notion of power is central, if we recall that hierarchies emanate from power). Choosing the theme of madness, Machado problematizes more than the pretentious scientific thought of his time. He works above all with the barrier that separates sanity from insanity, a decisive element for establishing the limits of madness and thus creating hierarchies. Once the limit is determined, the insane could be confined, and the sane would continue to be free.

José Carlos Garbuglio has pointed out the appropriateness of style to the creatures who confront each other in the novella:

on the one hand, a language that closes in on itself to express the world of the alienist, the austere scientist, "as cold as his diagnoses," "dispassionate as a god of stone"; on the other hand, "oratorical flights," "rhetorical voluptuousness," and semi-educated clichés used to describe the universe of superficial relationships ("Apresentação," 6), forms of expression so typical of the auditive orientation which, according to Luiz Costa Lima, is one of the peculiarities of the Brazilian intellectual system (*Dispersa demanda,* 15–26).

Here, making a slight adjustment, I would say that it is impossible to delimit clear territories in the text. The alienist Simão is also fascinated by flashy and verbose sayings ("till now, madness has been thought a small island in an ocean of sanity. I am beginning to suspect that it is not an island at all but a continent" [19; 9])[1] but maintains an enigmatic and circumspect pose only to impress others as a bulwark of science. He does not exactly oppose the other characters, using his rhetoric to preserve his own power in Itaguaí.

We can complete the analysis by recalling Alfredo Bosi's correct observation that the novella's axis is the arbitrary nature of power rather than the capriciousness of a mad scientist. Simão has always been on the side of the powerful. To conclude his task of separating the mad from the sane, he has to determine what constitutes normality. As Bosi notes, the story indicates that the normal is "something homogeneous repeated to the infinite. The normal is the pure form of public appearance," that which is "instituted without surprises." For this reason, "it is necessary to separate from public life all those who differ in some way from the established norm, from the dominant appearance," Bosi adds ("A máscara e a fenda," 443, 444). Suppressing difference is a violent form of arbitrariness and authoritarianism.

Movement on the level of the enunciated occurs, consequently, in the sense of annulling difference and perpetuating a complete uniformization in Itaguaí. Simão Bacamarte exercises power through knowledge, and despite the aborted revolt of the Canjicas, he is always in control and is never effectively challenged. Throughout the novella, oriented by this axis, there parades a gallery of human frailties: Dona Evarista's obsession with luxury, the saddler's ostentation, the fawning apothecary's moral torture, hesitating between staying in Bacamarte's shadow or joining the victorious rebels.

Hierarchies are contested even if one limits oneself to the dimension just outlined. The alienist, with his arrogance and dubious "scientific" parameters, installs a reign of terror, "unrestrained internment," culminating with the confinement of almost the entire population of the city. Then, changing the rules, he confines those blessed with moral qualities. The therapy ministered finally empties the Casa Verde and, having discovered the perfect disequilibrium of mental faculties, Bacamarte interns himself. How can one impose rigorous limits, if the alienist is the one who is alienated?

On the level of the enunciation—in the folds of the text—the critique goes even deeper. In chapter 3, Dona Evarista, Simão's wife, feels "as much a widow now as before she married him" (16; 7). The alienist then suggests that she take a trip to Rio de Janeiro and says that they have earned a lot of money with the half-dozen lunatics he has been treating. He then shows her the books: an opulent "milky-way of algorisms." Simão Bacamarte's high scientific proposals are unmasked through language itself, since with this expression he confesses his pecuniary interests.

The barber Porfírio revolts against the scientific despotism of the tyrannical alienist but feels the ambition to govern awake within him. Once the Canjicas are triumphant, Porfírio pulls out his sword, "as dexterously as if it had been merely an unusually long razor" (36; 26). By using language in this way, Machado sharpens the critical scalpel with which he implodes the deepest motivations of his characters: behind the revolutionary ideal, Porfírio was motivated by the desire for power.

The narrator does not explicitly assume a specific position in relation to what he narrates. One perceives the critical corrosion through language; writing itself is charged with denouncing the effects of bombastic oratory and the moral weakness of the various characters. The narrator, in fact, does not entirely adopt a single narrative version, since he always alludes to what the chronicles of Itaguaí say, whose vision of facts is conflictive. In this sense, the story puts a monolithical interpretation in check, allowing a plurality of meanings to circulate within it. If, therefore, on the level of the enunciated the text tends toward the authoritarianism of uniformity and the already established (which are shattered), on the level of the enunciation it tends toward a polysemy of interpretations.

Finally, besides maintaining an intertextual relationship with the scientific discourse or the shallow and exhibitionist rhetoric of the period, "The Psychiatrist" dialogues parodically with the French Revolution, which is displaced in colonial Itaguaí and reduced to the dimension of the Canjicas, as the rebels commanded by Porfírio were known. Porfírio, in fact, refers to the Casa Verde as the "Bastille of human reason" (31; 21). It would suffice to point to the titles of some chapters, such as "The Terror" and "The Restoration." Obviously, given the "difference between Paris and Itaguaí" and the reduction of proportions, which is clear in the epithet used to describe the rebels, the reader will perceive that the Revolution of 1789 is here reread parodically, acquiring other meanings.[2]

"The Psychiatrist" is but one example by which I hope to suggest, based on the formal innovations of Machado's writing, the de-hierarchical face of his fiction, which I believe to be his greatest innovation in the nineteenth-century Brazilian novel. Despite not going beyond the milieu of the ruling elites—never dealing, in this sense, with dominated sectors or with the dialectic of class struggle—Machado de Assis focuses on the dominant segments in a caustic manner. His literature, written during nearly a half-century, which ranges thematically from the colonial period to the beginning of the Republic, with more specific focus on the twilight of the Second Reign, is a portrait of nineteenth-century Brazilian society inside out.[3]

Machado's work, of high aesthetic voltage, concomitantly, without prejudicing its universalist implications, performs a detailed biopsy on Brazil of the late nineteenth century and foreshadows, with its modern narrative structure, a *transition* in Brazilian society. In effect, in a novel such as *Quincas Borba,* Machado's narrator confronts the provincial Rubião with a new, moneyed bourgeoisie that ends up devouring the protagonist, who, in a concretization of the parable that the philosopher had told him, is incapable of manipulating the rules of the Court's social game. Machado's eminently transgressive blade slices deep into the turn-of-the-century, surprising the emergence of the urban and nouveaux riches sectors that will dispute the exclusivity of power with declining oligarchies in the 1930s.

The Carpenter of Letters —An Intellectual Profile of Humberto de Campos

The limits of a book are, for me,
the limits of the universe.
—*Humberto de Campos*

I have done nothing that is solid and lasting.
—*Humberto de Campos*

I

The period between 1850, the date of the final prohibition of slave traffic (the first law, from 1831, was ignored), and the Revolution of 1930 is perhaps one of the most important for understanding the complexity of the Brazilian historical process. Although the definitive extinction of the slave trade would only occur later, with that measure there began a series of shocks that the country's archaic, agrarian, patriarchal, and seignorial social structure received in its passage toward a more urban society characterized by industrialization, urbanization, and a greater presence of middle sectors in the country's political life.

As we know, the empire's economy was based on slave labor, transforming the Second Reign, in the final analysis, into an enormous seignorial fazenda. The interests of the coffee barons were assured by the emperor's moderating power as well as by the councilors and lifelong senators who adulated them. When the pillars of slavery sustaining the bankrupt system were removed and the cracks in the nation's somnolent stability widened with military and religious disputes, abolition provided the final blow to the staggering monarchy. The abolitionist campaign and the rise of republican ideas (the Republican Manifesto dates from 1870), weakened the corroded foundations of the Second Reign so much that a military protest was sufficient to overthrow the monarchy.[1]

This process cannot be isolated from the international conjuncture. With the so-called Second Industrial Revolution, which improved manufacturing techniques, there occurred a startling increase in European production. Internal consumer markets could not absorb the excess, and overproduction affected the system's stability. A new imperialism then turned toward peripheral nations, forcing open new markets in the old empire and in precapitalist economies. Converted into a wage laborer, the former slave became a potential consumer. This invasion of European capital in dependent nations subordinated them to the industrial expansion and relegated them to the subaltern position of providers of the raw materials needed to sustain the high degree of industrialization reached by hegemonic countries. As a consequence of economic domination, the European style of life and cultural models were widely disseminated, standardizing human societies and molding them to the forms of behavior in fashion in the Old World.

Consequently, we should not think of the coup of 1889 without considering external pressures. Even summarily analyzing the confrontation of political forces at play, one sees that the class fractions who were victorious on November 15 joined with the interests of foreign monopolies. The Republic was possible thanks to a division in the dominant class, a split between the old landowners (notably those of the Paraíba Valley), still tied to slavery, and coffee growers (the fazendeiros from western São Paulo), who espoused new agricultural techniques and embraced capitalist relations of production, using a free labor force frequently composed of immigrants. The coffee growers, receptive to reformist ideas such as abolition and republicanism, allied themselves with bourgeois middle sectors such as the military (strengthened as a result of the Paraguayan war), civil servants, nascent industrialists, bankers associated with foreign capital, and intellectuals. The industrialists and bankers would later form an even more solid pact with enterprising São Paulo fazendeiros. Because they descended from the monarchical aristocracy or from decadent patriarchal families of the Northeast, intellectuals continued to be tied to the old order by affective relations, which explains the fact that behind their modern façade, they closed ranks with elitist and traditional positions.

The accord between those dominant progressive sectors from western São Paulo and the middle fractions led to the fall of the Empire and lasted until the moment when modernizing landowners competed for hegemony, discarding their allies, including intellectuals, and attempted a recomposition of the landed elites through the política dos governadores (the alternation in power of presidents from Minas Gerais and São Paulo) and the renewed dominance of oligarchies. The most conservative segment of the São Paulo coffee growers took control of power.

Intellectuals provided the ideology that the ruling classes need to mold a government according to their interests, free from the anachronistic monarchic machinery which was resistant to the progress demanded by modern times. The first attempt at the reformulation of Brazilian thought occurred with the positivism and scientific principles of the Recife School, whose primary figures were Tobias Barreto and his illustrious disciple, Sílvio Romero. Almost all of the period's intellectuals, fascinated by liberal and democratic ideas in their desire for modernization, joined in the abolitionist cause and the republican campaign.

Once proclaimed, the Republic initiated a painful process of social readjustment. A series of political crises, marked by dismissals and deportations, targeted not only traditional elites and their vast clientele, but also those who were most in tune with popular anxieties. The regime attempted to purify itself by purging the most exalted elements, who overflowed with republican ideals, as well as those who demonstrated little sympathy for the institutions implemented by the military coup of 1889. Neither excess nor lack of zeal was permitted.

Considering this filtering process, the boom and bust cycle of economic speculation known as the Encilhamento, with its numerous shady business deals, decreed the end of old fortunes and the sudden enrichment of citizens without a tradition of wealth, causing an alternation of elites. The final result of the new order's sedimentation was an open conservatism in the ideological sphere, together with material greed and the appearance of the nouveau riche and elegant bourgeoisie as prototypes of the dominant social ideal.

The same distillation process occurred in the federal capital. The urbanization of Rio de Janeiro during the administration of the "dictator" mayor Pereira Passos made it the country's greatest cosmopolitan center. The operation was popularly called the Bota Abaixo (Knockdown). It consisted of the demolition of the large old houses that had become hovels inhabited by the poor in order to open broad avenues (the Avenida Central was inaugurated in 1904) and beautify the city's center with squares and gardens, decorated with statues imported from Europe. The renewal was restricted neither to visual and urbanistic aspects nor to the eradication of epidemics with the promulgation of the law of compulsory vaccination, also in 1904. The Regeneration of the capital sought to disinfect the central part of the city, removing the poor and beggars to distant suburbs and hillsides, reserving the center for the chic and elegant whose favored promenade was the fashionable Rua do Ouvidor.[2] The destruction of the city's old physiognomy complemented the disappearance of the old imperial society in an authentic social cleansing. Serenades and public guitar playing were repressed; carnival was to be well behaved, in European style with Pierrots, Columbines, and Harlequins, yet nothing of popular costumes, drumbeats, or merrymakers.

The sweaty, poorly dressed, and barefoot people were despised, and metaphors of cleanliness, hygiene, and sanitation were common in the writing of the period's mundane columnists. The patriarchal and aristocratic austerity of dark clothes, frock coats, and top hats were exchanged for the lighter colors of the cashmere coat and the straw hat. The elites who attained power during the Regeneration developed new social habits, the most important of which was to be up-to-date with the latest fashions. The fever of consumerism thus competed with yellow fever.

On the political front, the construction of a Brazilian nation-state was proposed, inspired by liberal ideas and a blind belief in the power of science. It was believed that rationality would lead to material progress, peace, well-being, and prosperity. The intellectuals who participated in these changes and embraced such illusions ended up, however, standing on the side of the road. Instead of seeing an urban, industrial bourgeois society, based on the precepts of liberalism and reason and shaped by European models, what developed was a façade hiding the other face of Brazil, which continued to be rural and agrarian and led by authoritarian and "illiberal" oligarchs, still resting in the ecstasy of their "splendid cradle" without allowing the breezes of rationalism to disturb their sleep.

Intellectuals invested their energies in the Republic that they had helped create, functioning as catalysts for a historical transformation in the hope of being rewarded with positions of leadership for which they felt qualified. Their ideal triumphed, but events frustrated their expectations and took another path. Instead of reason, knowledge, and competence setting the tone (the country governed by the cream of talented men), the marketplace became the privileged and sacred value. In this context, intellectuals became socially useless personages, "musketeers without a mission," in Nicolau Sevcenko's felicitous synthesis.[3] The dream of the Republic ran aground in "coffee-with-milk politics" resulting from the pact among governors. In the most retrograde sense, once the rough edges provoked by republican commotion had been smoothed out, the ruling classes tied to the production and export of coffee allied themselves with the old, regional oligarchies, and, arm in arm with international capital, used the new institutions to maintain Brazil as an extensive seignorial fazenda. As one of Machado de Assis's sagacious characters notes, the nation had witnessed a "change of signboards."

II

Visitors to the Municipal Theater in Rio de Janeiro will note its similarity to the Opéra in Paris, its neoclassical majesty and its affiliation—evident in the inscriptions, the arabesques, the lighting, the interior design, the marble, and the furnishings—with a European cultural tradition of Parisian inspiration. In one of the front side rooms on the first floor are mural paintings representing Greece, Rome, Spain, and the Orient, each marked by exoticism, restrained sensuality, and the stereotyped images that idealize these cultures.

Despite the concern in some works of the turn of the century with knowing Brazilian reality in more critical and less idealistic and romantic parameters (I am thinking, for example, of Euclides da Cunha's *Os sertões* [1902]), cultural production of the first decades of the twentieth century, illustrated by the Municipal Theater's architecture (built in 1906–1909), tended to be contaminated by the germs of a fixation on Paris. Intellectuals looked toward European culture for a formula capable of awakening Brazil from its lethargic mental backwardness, placing it on the vertiginous tracks of progress and modernity. Within these coordinates, all reminders of the standards and costumes of traditional society were eliminated, just as popular culture was prevented from staining this cosmopolitan and mundane project identified with fin-de-siècle Paris. Once again, a process of sanitation, this time in the cultural arena.

Once it was clean and the poor and beggars expelled, the bourgeois could enjoy the Avenida Central, exhibit their exaggerated elegance and self-esteem, and appreciate the monuments that enhanced their desire to be European in Brazil, the supreme ambition of this tropical belle époque. Whereas in the baroque architecture we note a mixture of native and European ingredients in a still hesitant gesture of anticolonial, mestizo revolt, and whereas, after Independence, the elites sought to Brazilianize themselves by idealizing the Indian, their effort now is toward cultural purification, exorcising the spurious impurities that could stain their desire for cultural aryanism. It would not be exact to say that the architecture of the Municipal Theater is not Brazilian because of the absence of "Brazilianness": for the educated people of the period, Brazilianness was precisely like this, filtered, sanitized, and purified.[4]

If some intellectuals were sheltered under official, bourgeois cloaks (the most successful among them would be Coelho Neto), others were frequently critical of the regime (Euclides da Cunha and Lima Barreto). The bohemian life-style no longer had a place, and most writers hoped to enjoy the tranquillity of a public service position, to build a home and raise a family. The case of Aluísio Azevedo is typical: he suddenly ceased writing when he settled into a diplomatic career. Recalcitrant bohemians were denied entrance into the select pleiad of the Academy. Nevertheless, supported or not in the bosom of the status quo, the fact is that intellectuals enjoyed an uncommon prestige, wrapped in an aura of glory. At the same time, their critical and creative firepower decreased, when it was not completely annulled, either by cooptation or by manipulating literature for the purpose of social mobility and benefiting materially from their status as writers, making literary creation a frivolous and innocuous activity, no more than a form of leisure.

The process of urbanization provides the tone for the cultural atmosphere: the façade is all-important. Literature becomes banal, a situation aggravated by the proliferation of means of mass communication, particularly the newspaper. The small reading public, composed primarily of women, is poorly educated, although it is fascinated by ornamental, copious, and ostentatious discourse. On the other hand, the writer is no longer a member or client of the landed elites, close to the center of power, as had occurred in the previous century. His social condition changed, the support of the monarchical State disappeared, and intellectuals became an isolated category, frequently having to struggle for survival by competing in the market society. This explains in part why practically all were journalists or polygraphs, dedicating their efforts to several genres at the same time. Since writers could not live by their writing alone, other activities such as teaching or public positions, obtained by way of contacts and the prestige of being an intellectual, appeared in the curricula of many of the period's best-known names.

Another element that contributed to minimizing the critical potential of intellectual activity derives from the fact that a large part of the period's intelligentsia was composed of descendants of seignorial families in decline. Their biographies are frequently marked (and the coincidence deserves further exploration) by the death or material bankruptcy of the father, a gap that affects the perpetuation of the patriarchal order. According to Sérgio Miceli, these intellectuals maintain a secondary link to ruling fractions through kinship or patronage. Studying their memoirs and autobiographies, Miceli notes that their choice of an intellectual career results from some difficulty that blocks their access to the professions that lead to dominant positions. Thus, the intention of regaining social prestige—lost with the dequalification deriving from the decadence of the great, patriarchal families—made many of them pursue a literary career. That is, rather than being a visceral option, an activity that pretends to question the sociocultural context and contribute to the improvement of society and human life, we have a compensatory sublimation, undermined in its foundations from the outset.

Being educated meant having status. It was equivalent to not being backward, dependent, and ignorant. Since they did not need to provide specialized labor for consolidating the hegemonic sectors' dominance, because only the bureaucracy demanded some limited qualifications, schools and education were alienated from the surrounding reality. Schools served neither to teach the dominated to obey the dominant, nor to prepare the latter to exercise domination. In Florestan Fernandes's conclusive words, the consequence is that

> the "educated" and "enlightened" sectors converted education into a mere symbol of a social and cultural situation. As a means of mobility, middle sectors began to pursue education for the same reason, to show off and to obtain the social recognition of the increase in social prestige, but rarely to use it as the mechanism of social ascension itself. Finally, popular sectors remained at the margin of both processes, since for them education could not be manipulated as a social symbol, and the teaching schools provided did not, by itself, stimulate enthusiasm for learning. (*Educação e sociedade no Brasil,* 92–93)

In part due to the lack of universities, whose effective implantation and dissemination in Brazil dates from the 1930s, the great majority of the period's intellectuals were self-taught, in the sense that they had no specific education to produce the knowledge transmitted by their works. Nevertheless, they attended the existent law faculties, whether they graduated or not, a sufficiently long time to be injected with the virus of vacuous, rhetorical academic discourse. Hollow erudition would be the most salient characteristic of their knowledge. They were devourers of books, addicted to citations in Latin or French, but their voluminous indigestion did not result in interpretive analysis and synthesis. Rather, writers always understood what they swallowed through their voracious reading in its most episodic and superficial aspects. Their Hellenic fixation, their orientalism, their obsession with Paris, and their taste for proper language reveal the traces of a caste system. They thus cultivated their superiority in an attempt to make up for the neutralization of their social role.

Their pure Portuguese distinguished them from the common

people, whose speech was base and quotidian. Hellenism cleansed them intellectually of the stigma of being of mixed blood, and they felt that their cultivation of aryanization whitened them (again the purifying process of sanitization). Their mania for Greek and Latin culture is purely decorative, a "pasteboard Hellenophilia," in the words of Brito Broca. These intellectuals "hellenized by hearsay" (Broca), since no one could be judged educated without citing some Greek or a half-dozen words in Latin. Their vision of Paris was superficial, one more fashion. Their orientalism was that of a bazaar. There was no vertical questioning. It was a flowery, pompous culture, totally without instrumentality, to be shown on the Rua do Ouvidor, in the cafés and the salons. Literary life, closed groups, the gossip of the Academy, and the byzantine nature of oratory outweighed literature as such.

This cultural emptiness reached both production and consumption. Educated readers prayed to the same sonnet, and they adored these true idols and mystified literary stars. If intellectuals in fact undertook a specific role, it was this one, feeding the daydreams, the bovarism, and the superfluousness of the belle époque public with their leisurely chronicles and exotic poems. No stimulus for serious reflection. Literature conferred status and thus permitted a relative social ascension. It was not thought of as a discourse that transgressed and problematized the frontiers of reality. The period's writers, when television, sports, and popular music did not exist or were in their infancy, corresponded to the leading actors of soap operas, to soccer stars and race drivers, and to the singers of today's romantic ballads. The belle époque expressed the modernization of the most external aspects of the nation's sociocultural situation, reflecting the most advanced part of the country, those most at ease in the urban life-style of the large cities. City dwellers saw the other, rural Brazil as indolent and lazy.

Literature was supreme in cultural life. But it would be unnecessary to prick it to understand that it was wilted and spiritless—"society's smile." An already outdated neoparnassianism ruled a style fit for the dominant classes, with its virtuosic rhymes, its polished language, dripping with the trinkets of catchy phrases, and its witty aphorisms. A perfect target, in short, for the modernists, who, not by chance, would in their successful moments demand a mestizo culture and an "impure speech."[5]

III

Humberto de Campos's intellectual profile should rest on the sociohistorical support and the portrait of the intelligentsia drawn in broad strokes in the previous section. Going through the whole of his work and the ideas it expresses, one sees that he lived his time in contradictory fashion, in a period characterized by contradictions.

Born in Miritiba, a small town in the interior of Maranhão, the boy Humberto became an orphan very early in life, thus inscribing himself in the biographical constant referred to above, which obliged him to work from childhood. His father, it is worth noting, had "an unequivocal taste for letters," which he doubtless instilled in his son. To help in his family's subsistence, Humberto worked as a clerk in a relative's store. In his daydreams he imagined himself a partner of the firm, with his name on the store's signboard, in a dream of grandeur and importance. It did not yet occur to him to have his name on a book cover, but the thirst for recognition and social prestige had already touched him.

Such celebrities as Sousândrade visited the store. Local poets were "guests of honor," and the notoriety of a Coelho Neto—with whom Humberto de Campos later became close friends—came to Maranhão. In *Memórias inacabadas,* we read: "To be one day like Coelho Neto would be to receive a sign of immortality" (143). Literature as a form of evasion ("I would go to bed dreaming of the people who lived in books" [153]) excited the boy's imagination, which was also touched by the desire for glory that literature provided.

Nonetheless, the adult Humberto de Campos experienced both consecration and its decline. He notes in his *Diário secreto* that a survey undertaken by the press in São Paulo rated him the most widely read author of the period. He became a member of the Brazilian Academy of Letters, enjoyed the friendship of the most brilliant men of politics and culture, served as a federal deputy from his native state, and left a vast work exceeding forty volumes. The advent of Modernism, on the aesthetic plane, and the Revolution of 1930, on the sociopolitical front, seemed to remove the foundations on which he based his existence, aggravated by poverty and by illness that led to his death. Humberto de Campos suffered from an enlargement of the pituitary gland, provoked by a tumor, with complications in the bladder and the prostate as well as such collateral effects as dormancy of the hands, the inability to have sexual relations, and, finally, blindness. The writer dedicated many pages to his physical suffering and his difficulty in providing for his family with his occupation as a "proletariate of the pen."

This, in fact, is a complaint that recurs in Humberto de Campos's writing. Instead of the great work that he had imagined, necessity forced him to dissipate his efforts in crônicas of little value. On one occasion he even wrote thirty-seven newspaper articles in just eighteen days. For this reason, instead of planting "expensive trees that produce only after five years," "he planted common legumes that bear fruit in five weeks" (cited by Machado Neto, 77), instead of "making a majestic and solid piece of furniture," this "carpenter of letters" saw himself compelled to sell, each morning, the board he had planed the night before (*Os párias*, 24). One sees clearly that the changes of his social situation affected him drastically, making him—and this is his argument—write a numerous and vast, yet circumstantial, oeuvre, far less than the monument he hoped to raise, one that would be worthy of a man of letters.

Humberto de Campos's literary and aesthetic preferences are easily extracted from his texts. In Coelho Neto, for whom he nurtured unconditional admiration, he praised the "powerful imagination" and the fervent "cult of letters" ("O aniversário de Coelho Neto," in *Sepultando os meus mortos*).[6] In Olavo Bilac he appreciated the classicism, the admirable verses, the poetry that "represents, by itself, a chapter in our literary history" ("Olavo Bilac," in *Fatos e feitos*). In Paulo de Frontin, Pereira Passos's right-hand man in the construction of the Avenida Central, he exalted the "astonishing engineer," the "entrepreneurial genius" of a true titan, suited to modern ebullience (*Perfis*, first series). On the other hand, witnessing the city's transformation, he expressed nostalgia for the euphoric days of the belle époque when he arrived in Rio in 1912.

In "O espírito francês" (*Fatos e feitos*), Campos exalts the charming French people and their elegant gentility, considering Paris "the living room of the modern world." This apparent adherence to the new times goes against his reverence for the classical order, which, in his *Memórias*, he attributes to his probable Portuguese descent. However, although he so fervently places himself in the tradition of erudite knowledge, from time to time there appears in his texts the man from Miritiba, Maranhão, attracted to folkloric expression such as Bumba-meu-boi or the simplicity of a Catulo da Paixão Cearense.

Nevertheless, although he praises Catulo's popular poetry, in flagrant contrast he does so in a language saturated with Parnassianism. Humberto de Campos finds himself caught between the song thrush (sabiá) and the cacique (xexéu) inscribed in the title of one of his crônicas (*Da seara de Booz*): despite dedicating it "to a Greco-Latin scholar who knew neither Greek nor Latin," it seems to fit his dilemma perfectly. Between the eclectic "polyphonic voice" of the cacique, which "picks up everything," including the voices of a universe that no longer exists and which it had in fact never heard, and the nationalism of the song thrush, which wants its mate to be a bird of his forest and trees, we can recognize the cultural contradictions Campos suffered.

Humberto de Campos was a devourer of books and an assiduous reader of classical writers. In contrast, however, to what he recommended in a crônica of *Mealheiro de Agripa,* he does not seem to have been parsimonious in the ingestion of other texts. Consequently, the critique he makes of the urban critics who write about Catulo da Paixão Cearense without knowing the sertão seems, again, to be tailor-made for himself: since he also traveled "on the spine of books," "on the saddle of others," in the sense that he always understood what he had read in episodic terms, without a more perceptive critical evaluation. He thus could not avoid the false erudition which was the trademark of the intellectuals with whom he is associated. In his crônicas, for example, he would start with a fact of everyday life and immediately compare it with another, invariably citing an author or text from the Greco-Latin or European tradition or the Bible (or vice versa). I illustrate this tendency with a passage from "O defunto vaiado" (*Os párias*), in which he traces the figure of the boxer Primo Carnera, "more a monster than a man": "placed among the Greeks before besieged Ilion, he would not cut a bad figure among Homer's warriors. He would have the legs to challenge Antilochus in races and the arms to shoot arrows with Teucer, throw javelins with Meriones, and the high and distant discus like Epeus or Polybotes. With his jawbone Samson would have defeated more Philistines than with that of his ass. A brother of that Cleomedes of whom Plutarch speaks, he would have broken, like him, pillars and destroyed edifices" (149–50).

In his need to legitimize his writing by establishing a European textual lineage, showing off his knowledge and readings, Humberto de Campos does not realize that the underlying contexts are different, nor does he recognize the dangers of hurriedly moving from one text to another without precautions. When he exclaims "blessed be Allah and his Prophet, who in Arabia thirteen centuries ago enacted so many excellent things for Brazil," or when he judges that "what would be resolved today with the heads of four men could have been resolved twenty-six centuries ago with the head of a single woman" (*Mealheiro de Agripa*, 145, 140), he reveals himself to be inconsequential, jumping from one sociohistorical circumstance to another. He also expresses a repetitive and circular conception of time, without seeing ruptures and differences in the flow of History and without perceiving the fictive nature implicated in the sources to which he alludes.

In this sense, Humberto de Campos shares the same posture as other intellectuals of the period, armed, like them, with Hellenism, orientalism, and Francophilia. His creations do not avoid, moreover, the moralizing tone that pervades both the crônicas and the humorous stories, the children's literature and oriental tales, as well as his memoirs. In the preface to the latter he writes: "To those who have gone to sea or are far away, I have come to bring a hand, a light, and a compass" (*Memórias*, 7). In another passage, from "Aos meus amigos da Bahia" (*Sombras que sofrem*), he attributes to the poor writer, in a poor country, the mission of condemning errors, spreading goodwill, and sowing truth. The intellectual, above common mortals and blessed with knowledge and culture, should orient the naive and disoriented reader, a position with political repercussions, as we will soon see.

In relation to prototypical characteristics of a man of letters in the first decades of the century, Humberto de Campos shows astuteness by ironizing certain common forms of his generation's behavior, such as the showiness and oratorical vacuousness of public speakers, with the lecture being the fashion of literary life of so-called premodernism, or, further still, the dubious criteria with which poets were elected to a chair in the Academia, satirized allegorically in "A rã e o sabiá" (*Pombos de Maomé*).

Concomitantly, with his fidelity to the European cultural past, Humberto de Campos is uneasy with the question of nationalism. It is worth reading how, according to him, Coelho Neto understood the problem by initiating a campaign against the adoption of the acanthus leaf as an emblem on military uniforms: "We have elements for a national aesthetic inspired by the shape of our leaves, by the contour of our palm trees, by the profile of our mountains. What do we have to do with the laurel leaf? What does an acanthus plant mean to us? What place do the oak tree, the shade of the poplar, the fruit of the mulberry, the song of the nightingale have in our history? We should speak of the macaw, the mango, the banana tree, the Surinam cherry, the song thrush, the parrot, and the oriole" (*Gansos do Capitólio,* 366–67).

This packaged nationalism, which everything leads us to believe that Humberto de Campos accepted and which stresses the exotic, a mere exchange of labels, is far from answering the question of our cultural identity. We will not give Brazilian features to the Bible by substituting nettle for grape leaves, as Coelho Neto seems to suggest in this text. It is not by carrying the standard of the broa de milho (corn cake), as a Minister of Culture recently proposed, that we will preserve our patrimony or overcome cultural dependency. Within this line of reasoning, poems such as "Tempestade amazônica," "No sertão," or "O seringueiro" (*Poesias completas*) transpire "Brazilianness" only in the title.

Curiously, however, on confronting the barbarians of "modernist patrols," Campos recognizes that they undertook a thematic nationalization. In the days of the sonnet, the Parnassians always wrote about identical themes, using the same diction, and, after reading a book of verse, it was almost impossible to determine the author's background. The opposite began to occur with the "undisciplined battalion of modernist poets," to the extent that Modernism "made every poet the expression of his environment, the voice of his people, if not in technique, at least in language and themes" (*Crítica,* second series, 286). Campos thus captures the song thrush rather than the cacique facet of part of the first modernist generation.

In "A defesa de Noé" (*Reminiscências*) he clearly affirms his position: he is not a modern spirit, but rather an ancient among ancients. Such is his profession of faith. A serene ancestor among the clamor of youth, defending tradition against the young hordes of modernist vandals. To set forth his position in the face of the avalanche unleashed by the Week of Modern Art, Humberto de Campos undertakes a long and erudite incursion in the article "A poesia nova" (*Crítica,* second series) to show that classical culture emerged from the tomb in which it had been buried during the Middle Ages, under the stones of eight centuries, to awake luxuriant in the Renaissance. How, he asks, could this rich patrimony fall before the "war cry of a small group of nice young men," before iconoclastic screams of "down with Greece" and "out with Latins"? Humberto de Campos reserves to himself the role of the "last of the Hellenes," the bulwark of the classical tradition against the modernist invasion.

Campos thus received Modernism ambivalently. In a passage of the second volume of his *Diário secreto,* he explains to Coelho Neto's wife, Dona Gabi, the reason for her husband's diminished brilliance: "The new generation, the generation that succeeded his and mine, speaks another language from ours and cannot understand us. We cultivated the art of writing well, we made style a religion; the barbarians are there to destroy what we adored, we speak a language they do not understand; we are foreigners among them [. . .]. Our classical spirit and our love for ancient culture, disdained by the present generation, make each of us a creature of a Lost World" (168).

Campos experiences the same sensation of an "antediluvian being" in relation to the Revolution of 1930. In *Os párias* he affirms that "they knocked him from the scaffold when he was working on the building of the Old Republic" (28). In the *Diário secreto* he calls Getúlio Vargas a "laughing fool." In his opinion, in 1931 the country was submerged in disorganization and reduced to misery, no longer appreciating the labor of writing, inverting the dominant practice of the golden belle époque. In his criticism of the revolutionary process detonated in 1930, Humberto de Campos put his finger on the wounds and misfortunes of our political habits, believing that the New Republic was going along the same path as the Old. In "Elogio de uma conduta" (*Notas de um diarista*) he asks that amnesty be given the regime's opposition and that exceptional measures be revoked. His understanding of Brazilian revolutions is transmitted with extreme perspicacity in the fable titled "No mosteiro de São Malaquias" (*Pombos de Maomé*).

Campos's social and political thought is found in "Uma voz na sombra" (*Os párias*), when he answers a woman who had expected him to become a communist. In this text it is clear that his concern with the lower classes is purely sentimental, with no serious or penetrating coloration. For Humberto de Campos, the way to attack the bourgeoisie would be provisionally to eliminate freedom. "Only dictatorship," he writes, "or, more precisely, tyranny, can do something for the proletariat in today's world" (11). He believes that full freedom among poor people is more "vanity than necessity" (18). Elsewhere he noted: "Freedom is a poison, like that of Mithridates: to use it, one must prepare the organism to receive it with a patient, centuries-long education. It is first necessary to shape the armor of character to enable it to carry this weapon, which always harms those who fall under its weight" (*Crítica,* second series, 234).

As measures intended to ease the red threat among the working classes, he suggests interesting them in the "prosperity of the factories," which would mean, and the paradox is evident, making them work in favor of capital and against themselves. He further prescribes the strange "preventive medicine" of giving more bread than freedom, in a well-known ideological attitude which nourishes a paternalistic sympathy for the oppressed and scarcely hides its intentions of keeping them calm and dominated, with pieces of bread pacifying their grievances and revolt.

Campos notes the progressive degradation of the Brazilian black, which he attributes to the "political error of abolition." As he understands it, the black of his time is more socially worthless than during the days of slavery, despite the opportunities that whites offer him. In parallel terms, he perceives that the whites' false fraternity is destroying the black. His conclusion deserves to be emphasized: the black race no longer produces "champions of freedom," bathed in sun and glory (*Contrastes,* 23, 24), having abandoned the schoolroom to go out in the streets during carnival, dressed like baianas (Bahian women).

The man of the backlands is personified in the figure of the cangaceiro Lampião, blessed with the epithets of the "most terrible murderer," "Brazil's worst disgrace," "a backlands calamity," in sum, a "social cancer" (*Notas de um diarista,* first series). Behind the "wild acts of the bandit" Campos is unable to see the marginalization to which the rural population of the countryside had been condemned, buried by the steamroller of "progress." Regarding women, Campos's work was attentive to the accentuated emergence of feminism, recognizing, for example, in the entanglements of narratives about adultery that appear in his crônicas and short stories, the importance of the woman's sexual satisfaction. However, the author's eventual foresight slips in passages such as this, extracted from *Um sonho de pobre:* isn't fidelity "the woman's natural mission?" (70).

The politico-ideological position unveiled in Humberto de Campos's paternalistic attitude toward minority segments of society is clear. Our "carpenter of letters" was a partisan of a "philanthropic, educated, intelligent, and liberal tyranny" (*Os párias,* 12), without suspecting that the fact of being a tyrant deprives anyone of the illusion of being a true liberal. For him, in Russia, intellectuals led the Revolution, that is, educated men at the forefront of the process, "saving national integrity," the people's hand, light, and compass, a posture with which we are familiar: "It is necessary that a group of men of thought, transformed into men of action, elaborate the initial century of the new era of humanity. But where are such providential men?" (*Os párias,* 16). Humberto de Campos advocates a strong government—a "dictatorship of law"—managed by a caste of intellectuals, a sort of mandarinate, a reedition of enlightened despotism, which professed the "eclectic cult of knowledge" and an intelligent and liberal tyranny.

In a commentary on a book by Oliveira Vianna, he expands the principles that should orient the country's new constitution: a restricted vote, limitations on freedom, technocratic legislators, institutionalization of a state of siege. The example of Haiti, which had begun "to live in peace and plenty like a civilized land" after it had been enslaved by a North American invasion, is sufficiently symptomatic and eliminates any doubts one may have with respect to Campos's political convictions. The nostalgic vision with which he contemplates the weeds and the dilapidated houses, to which the prosperous fazendas and fruitful mills of days gone by have been reduced, is clear (*Crítica,* second series, 198–99). He is an intellectual ideologically bound to the decadent seignorial order that glimpsed, with the republican convulsions and in the name of the country's modernization, an opportunity to reassume a position of leadership in the lap of power, and which saw this project aborted as a capitalist model was followed instead of another one which would let itself be led by an intellectual elite. Instead of drawing a halo of glory, the pen becomes a way of life. Literature ceases being a priesthood to become an industry in a market society.

Consequently, Humberto de Campos lived the contradictions of his time in conflictive terms. He serves as a paradigmatic example of the migrant intellectual whose original cultural repertoire was swallowed up by urban cosmopolitanism, with a resulting loss of ties to his native region. Although he was not the creator of a production which took great flight or delved into the magma of the human condition or the clamor and social tensions that surrounded him—and in this he followed the "society's smile" tendency—Humberto de Campos's prolific bibliography serves witness, in its own way, to his epoch. His levity and elegant humor were healthy in the face of a conception of the intellectual or of literature as necessarily morose, sullen, and incapable of sense of humor. This quality was probably dictated in part by the demands of a reading public, composed especially of women, avid for amenities, with feminism having been one of his favorite topics. If, on the one hand, this lightness compromised the ambition to perpetuate his name, writing both what was useful to his contemporaries and what would stay in the people's memory, as he asserts in "Uma voz na sombra" (*Os párias*, 24–25), leaving the trail of his work to beyond his own death, on the other hand, it explains, to a great extent, his success. Again the contradiction between Demophile and Philocrite (cf. "A ilusão de Filócrito," *Lagartas e libélulas*), between acclamation in the present or laurels in the future—his true option is to have both.

Frivolity would also be partially responsible for Humberto de Campos being almost totally forgotten today. Since he is considered a minor writer, we must attempt to rescue him for today's readers so that he can be reevaluated in terms of current parameters of reading and taste. Criticism formed under the yoke of immanent analysis, deifying the text, belittles the role of consumption in literary creation and minimizes the writer's social status as an intellectual subject to the ideological injunctions of his time and class. Reacting against such a state of things, I suggest that an author who was so widely read deserves to be reexamined, evaluating the framework of his production in search of the contradictions and the sediments deposited in it by the knowledge and tensions of the epoch and world in which he lived.

Humberto de Campos crystallizes, in the paradoxes that permeate his thought and work, the prototypical intellectual of the belle époque surprised by the "change of signboards" of the Republic, by the Revolution of 1930, and by Modernism. It is necessary to bring him into the debate in order to formulate in a more congruent fashion the intellectual's insertion in society as well as to weigh more precisely the exact dimensions of a work that did not consist in "great, whole statues," having rather been shattered in pieces and dust; of a traveler who "did not climb mountains, where winds roar, nor descend into deep valleys, rich with mysteries," having limited himself to walk through "domestic gardens, along well-known roads, and planted fields." He said of himself: "If the marches were not longer and more beneficial, the blame does not belong entirely to him who undertook them. There were not enough hours in the day nor energy in the pilgrim" (*Crítica*, first series, "Prefácio," 12).

By commenting on some of the ideas in the work of Humberto de Campos, it is not my purpose to judge him. The greatest figures of Brazilian literature, such as Machado de Assis, are equally spattered with contradictions. Not having wanted to measure the "pilgrim's energy," I transfer the verdict to the reader. Concentrating on the intellectual and not the man, on the ideas and not the flesh and blood, it seemed important to use a certain lack of indulgence to the extent that many of Humberto de Campos's convictions, precisely those that are politically and culturally execrable to a more severe critical gaze, continue to be in fashion in Brazil. For those who, like him, still assign themselves the role of hand, light, and compass.

The Almond Tree and the Banana —Impotence in José Lins do Rego

The old almond tree withstood the wind with the tranquility of having its roots firmly in the ground.
—*José Lins do Rego*

I

José Lins do Rego's sugarcane cycle can be taken as paradigmatic, in the sense that it represents quite well the fictional model practiced during the period of *transition* in the 1930s. It relates the decadence of the rural seignorial system, the advent of sugar refineries, and the decay of the masculine and patriarchal orders, and also possesses a memorialistic substratum. In addition, it presents the disruption caused by a character who had studied in the city and who is no longer able to be an authentic senhor de engenho (sugar plantation owner). The protagonist depicted (and here fiction blends with biography, as evidenced by Lins do Rego's memoirs) is an intellectual who is socially disqualified by moving to the urban space and who attempts to regain his prestige by becoming a writer (Carlos de Melo plans a book about his grandfather). More importantly, it concerns an individual with difficult family relationships, notably with his father, a rather common phenomenon in the fictional characters, as well as among the writers and intellectuals, of the moment that interests this chapter.

An exhaustive analysis of Lins do Rego's work is beyond the scope of this study. Rather, starting with a rapid examination of some of his novels, I am interested in discussing the impotence that assails his protagonists. I hope to challenge a rather widespread opinion—and I am not the first to question it—according to which Lins do Rego's work can be considered one of social criticism. This revision should have consequences for a more realistic evaluation of the period's cultural production, particularly in its intersection with the discourses that constitute the historical context and in its implications for a greater understanding of Brazilian modernization.

In the portrait the narrator Carlos de Melo draws of his grandfather, Colonel José Paulino, we must consider the affective and sentimental bond that makes us read passages such as this with suspicion: "José Paulino ruled his plantation with benevolence" (72; 64);[1] "he was a feudal lord, but servitude did not lie heavy on the backs of these peasants" (76; 69). Suspicions of the opinions emitted by the grandson about the old patriarch, a "saint who planted sugarcane," are confirmed in the episode narrated in chapter 18 involving the mulatto girl Maria Pia and the slave Chico Pereira. The latter is accused of deflowering the girl, and Paulino orders him placed in shackles so he will confess and marry her. Such "justice" is ambiguous, since Maria Pia finally says that the one who had abused her was Juca, Paulino's son. At this moment, of course, nothing will happen, since Juca will neither get married nor be tortured. Two weights, two measures. They help us read the following passage with the proper ideological perspective: "I thought it quite natural to see them living and sleeping in a pigsty, having nothing to eat, and working like beasts of burden. My understanding of life at that time made me accept all this as part of God's plan. They had been born like this because God wanted it that way, just like God had wanted us to be white and to rule over them" (88; 80). If the detail of the affective bond does not annul, it at the very least minimizes the indictment occasionally present in the pages of this first novel.

The other fact that deserves mention with respect to *Menino de engenho* emerges from a comparison of the novel with *Meus verdes anos,* Lins do Rego's childhood memoirs. The work of fiction undergoes a process of condensation in relation to facts from the writer's biography. Both begin by narrating the experience of the death of the mother and loss of the father. In *Menino de engenho,* the father kills the mother and goes to an asylum, and the boy is raised by his aunt, whom he will lose when she gets married, and by his grandfather, who assumes the symbolic role of father. In *Meus verdes anos,* the writer's mother dies, and the boy is raised by an aunt and his grandfather. In the memoirs, the father's exclusion occurs because he does not belong to the clan. In other words, the life of the character Carlos (and of the novelist himself, I would add) is "marked by the destruction of the nuclear family," and the character's evolution occurs in such a way that the landowning family's ruin implies his degradation (Lopes, 66).

Curiously, in the Santa Rosa plantation mansion there is no marriage: José Paulino is a widower, Aunt Maria moves to her husband's plantation when she gets married, and Sinhazinha is separated. If we include *Fogo morto* in the analysis, we see that Colonel Lula de Holanda and Carlos's father are similar in the sense that women are who connect them to the family and to the process of succession on the plantation (Lopes, 81), which would suggest that the patriarchal and masculine lineage is weaker in them. Carlos resembles the saddlemaker Zé Amaro and Lula to the extent that their respective fathers are exceptional figures (82). As José Sérgio Leite Lopes has shown, the families of Santa Rosa and Santa Fé, as well as those of Zé Amaro and Colonel Lula de Holanda, present many common characteristics (80, 82). Lopes calls special attention to the fact that Lula's father-in-law Tomás, Lula himself, and Zé Amaro face the impossibility of reproducing themselves in the next generation, given the strangeness of their daughters (83). And, in the context of the sugar refinery there are no more women (84), which leads to the conclusion that "the family character of the plantations tends to disappear with the onset of refineries, which tend to be transformed into corporations" (84).

With respect to the family, the three texts mentioned above seem to start from the same point, since there are so many coincidences that affect characters such as Lula, Zé Amaro, Tomás, Carlos de Melo, and the author himself as a memorialist. Consequently, the fissures in the nuclear family not only compromise the structure of the plantation as an economic and social unity, permitting us to accompany its transition to the anonymous and less family-oriented nature of the refinery, but also point toward a weakening of the masculine and patriarchal orders along with the decline of the traditional agrarian system.

This is the context that underlies my reading of *Fogo morto* (1943), considered Lins do Rego's masterpiece. Spatial limitations impede me from reviewing all existent criticism about the novel,[2] but I will establish a dialogue and take issue with one of the most recent studies. In *O romance de 30,* José Hildebrando Dacanal writes that *Fogo morto* "presents a project for a new social order" (27). The basis of his argument rests on the detail that, in the chronology he establishes, based in the plots, this novel precedes the works that comprise the so-called sugarcane cycle. In comparison with them, what *Fogo morto* presents that is new "is precisely a conscious political revolt and a critical vision of the socio-economic structures of the world described, followed by the presentation of the ideal of a new, just and democratic political order, a presentation made through a character who seems to completely 'escape' the novelist's control and who changes from a grotesque individual to a much broader quixotic prototype, the personification of the immaculate hero, defender of the oppressed against all orders based on injustice" (33).

This character is obviously Captain Vitorino, seen by Dacanal as anachronistic, but through whom the novel articulates a "*critical vision of the world of the sugar mill and the plantation as well as of the economic, social and political conditions existing within them*" (34).[3] Later, after a digression that attempts to explain Papa-Rabo (Vitorino) as a representative of a liberal-democratic utopia, Dacanal seems to contradict himself by writing that "it is not with discourses based on vacuous rhetoric, with quixotic acts, with an external defense of democracy and egalitarianism that a society will defend the values of humanism and civilization" (40). If I read the passage correctly, it totally neutralizes any "project for a new social order" that could be transmitted through the Captain, since his revolt is innocuous and it occurs in the ambience of a rhetoric that is inflamed, but empty of efficacy and political force.[4]

I see *Fogo morto* as a large metaphor of the impotence of its characters, who belong to different social segments, to act and modify the reality that surrounds them. Master Zé Amaro, the saddlemaker, represents a productive yet still artisan force attempting to maintain his position, which distinguishes him from the lowest social sectors, in the face of decline (his father had made saddles for the Emperor) that circumstances force on him. Interiorizing certain values of the dominant fractions (he is, for example, a machista who blames his wife for not giving him a son), his indignation and revolt against Colonel Lula do not materialize, and he is limited to helping the cangaceiro (social bandit) Antônio Silvino, whom he idolizes.

When Colonel Lula de Holanda gets married, he becomes the senhor of Santa Fé. A delicate man of urban extraction, having been transplanted to the agrarian universe, he lacks the strong will necessary to run the plantation. His inadaptation and the impropriety of his leadership are reflected in his carriage and in the habit of prayer that he introduces. He is a banana, despite his cruelty to blacks.[5] Lula's failure in running Santa Fé is confirmed when his mother-in-law begins to give orders. In a masculine and patriarchal context, this violates social expectations. Coming from the city, Lula de Holanda is unable to avoid the plantation's inexorable demise.

Vitorino Papa-Rabo, belonging to a less-defined segment—he is neither a decadent colonel, like Lula, nor an all-powerful master, symbolized by José Paulino—could be seen as a kind of politician (he dreams of being mayor) whose participation rests on verbal rhetoric. Quixotic, taking his revolt to the extreme of cursing, Papa-Rabo's indignation is totally useless and, as in the cases of the other two characters, insufficient to alter the social situation drawn by the narrator. These three protagonists are consumed by impotence. Captain Antônio Silvino,[6] the cangaceiro, takes up arms against some of the powerful, but his subversive potential is emptied in violence and in a lack of organization and political consciousness. On the other side, also using armed violence, but this time in the name of order and a central power, is Lieutenant Maurício (he is spokesman for the State, then in the process of consolidation). The difference between him and Silvino is more of degree than of kind; both are used by the old bosses or the new mandarins of the system.

In *Fogo morto,* the character who continues manipulating the pieces of the political chessboard is Colonel José Paulino, fugacious but untouched by the narrative, revealing no signs of weakness or defeat. In one of his appearances, for example, his mere presence fills the room with respect (258).

Fogo morto questions more the "bad" and illegitimate colonel than the colonelistic system as a dynamic of power. It ultimately, and more or less implicitly, points toward the past rather than focusing on the present.[7] It suggests, furthermore, an alliance between the lieutenant and the bulwark of oligarchies—Maurício and José Paulino—in a fictionalization of the pact of 1930. The result is that both the Santa Fé plantation and the most important characters (the saddlemaker, Lula, and Vitorino) are characterized by "fogo morto" (dead fire), incapable of interfering in a transformative manner in a moribund social mechanism, which did not allow possibilities for effective changes capable of modernizing the society. Instead of being an indictment, José Lins do Rego's novel is a portrait of the apathy that seems to run through the Brazilian *transition,* in which a traditional order no longer has a historical existence and a bourgeois order has not yet been totally implanted. The eventual denunciation existent in the presentation of this apathy is compromised by the nostalgic character implicit in the author's fiction. This impasse, in which the past impedes the radical problematization of the present—which is that lived by the country's process of modernization[8]—appears on the horizon of *Fogo morto* and of most of the literature of the moment studied here.

II

I will now examine *Eurídice,* a novel practically ignored by critics, with the purpose of completing the analysis initiated with the discussion of *Fogo morto.* The psychoanalytical contours of *Eurídice* will affirm and supplement the arguments made in the previous section. Despite the fact that it abandons the Northeast with the sugar plantations and takes place in the urban context of Rio de Janeiro, an interpretation of this 1947 novel provides valuable support for understanding José Lins do Rego's fictional world and even sheds light on the sugarcane cycle, the most significant part of his work.

As in *Menino de engenho* and *Meus verdes anos,* the protagonist of *Eurídice,* Julinho, loses his father, at the age of eight. His father had been completely ruined (as was rather common with fathers of protagonists and in biographies of novelists in the 1930s): "Julinho came into the world to show my creditors that I was not as bankrupt as they supposed," says the father; to which his son, the narrator, adds: "I was thus the son of defeat," "I was born into a house dominated by failure" (32). It is curious to note further how material insolvency, which results in the loss of economic and especially social power, is compensated by the certification of virility the birth of a son provides. That is, the social, economic, family, and sexual levels mix together. It is in this atmosphere marked by impotence that Julinho is born, the son of elderly parents, an "embarrassment" rejected by his mother, who pushed him aside—the Julinho "of the caresses of my sisters, the severity of my mother, and the rudeness of my father," who grows up virtually abandoned (33).

Again, therefore, we have an affective lack and a conflictive relationship in the nuclear family, which is the origin of the problematic that affects both the narrator and, keeping in mind the memoirs and the recurrence of this scene (understanding the term in its psychoanalytical meaning), the writer himself.

The lack of esteem is filled by his sister Isidora, whom the boy desires in oedipal fashion. Consequently, he both hates and is jealous of her fiancé, Dr. Luís, when he catches his sister kissing him (the scene does not leave his mind [42]). Dr. Luís, perceiving the paternal hiatus in the family, becomes the absolute lord of both the house and Isidora (43). Thus the desire that takes hold of the protagonist to kill the usurper, who is stealing his coveted substitute mother. And thus his violent reaction, cutting Isidora's wedding dress (47).

The urban space lives under the legacy of the Brazilian agrarian and patriarchal past. In this eminently masculine context, the expectation is created that men will be strong and women docile. The novel consistently insists on this aspect of the character's personality, mixing social and economic power with masculinity and virility. Fontes, the uncle from the interior who visits the house in Tijuca, is weak. He had married Aunt Catarina "more to have a mother than a wife" (49). When Dr. Luís expels Jorge, he assumes a masculine attitude, "he was a man, he would give orders to Isidora, he would order us all," and Julinho feels like a weakling when faced with his rival's firmness in the dispute for his sister's love (103). Raised without a man in the house and to the liking of women who loved or scorned him—rejected by his mother (who made a gesture of repugnance when he kissed her hand [77]), he finds support on Isidora's lap—the protagonist feels like a poor, confused soul.

But in his affection for Isidora he confuses the sister, the mother, the wife and lover. Julinho's desire is evident: he remembers her kisses and embraces, and her "figure in the flesh, pale as white silk" is in his mind and later in his body (108). Feeling that he is losing her through her marriage to Dr. Luís, he wants to see her die during labor, which eventually happens, generating guilt and leaving the lack alive—the lack of the father, rejection by the mother, and now the death of the second mother.

The novel's title suggests that the narrative's central figure is Eurídice. The narrator-protagonist is incarcerated and proposes to tell the truth "as it really is." But to tell everything (about Eurídice and why he is in jail), he has to return to the past that seems "totally dead" (31) and narrate his experience from childhood, which occupies the entire first part of the novel. It is clear that Eurídice becomes inextricably linked to this past and to the family scene, rendered peculiar by the absence or harshness of the nuclear family's components and by the unfulfilled desire to fill this originary emptiness.

Thus, in the second part we find Julinho still weak, in search of a substitute for his primordial lack. His roommate, Faria, is a father to him (139). He needs a woman, and in a bordello he fails because Isidora's image invades him ("he saw Isidora in the venal woman who had given herself nude in bed" [169]). In his sexual desire he finally separates the pure from the impure, such as when he begins to like Noêmia and feels himself "above a swamp, above the mud" (173).

The object of his love will be finally concentrated in Eurídice, who comes to represent his lack with respect to feminine figures. To complicate the case further, one night she visits his friend Faria, who had been like a father to Julinho. With the two of them in bed, in the dark, all desires possessed the narrator-protagonist: "The more I knew that she belonged entirely to Faria, the more I was attracted to her flesh, to her body" (214). It would be superfluous to insist on the sick, alienated, and perverse character of this form of vicarious sexual satisfaction.

The narrator writes that Eurídice is the only woman who had no connection with the dead world of the past (207). Of course he is mistaken, not only because the past was not dead, since he had reconstructed it in the first part of the narrative, but also and more importantly because Eurídice has everything to do with this past, where the original situation that helped shape the protagonist's unconscious problematic resides. Eurídice herself does not matter as an individualized person (just as Isidora and Noêmia did not matter), but because she is an external manifestation of the psychic inscription of a *trace*—and in this sense, unveiled the text's unconscious—the title is appropriate since it remits to this originary mark. It is this mark, this trace, that he must tame. It is not gratuitous that in the moment before the murder, Eurídice's voice evokes in him "the harsh voice of my mother" (291), or that, at the very same moment when he strangles Eurídice, he feels in control, with hands of steel (292). By dominating her he attempts to affirm his power, his masculinity (in symbolic terms). This explains why subjugating Eurídice brings him pleasure. The following examples show the fusion of sexual desire and physical domination. In both, Eurídice is crying, a probable indication of weakness: "I looked at Eurídice, and, seeing her quiet, with her eyes wet with tears, and seeing her submissive, I felt as if I had imposed that submission. I grew stronger; the strength of dominance illuminated my eyes and gave me courage" (230); "my Eurídice, submissive, eyes filled with tears. Yes, I would have her in my arms, I would have her thighs, I would have her breasts. And right there, I felt an infernal desire to possess Eurídice. I wanted to run home and have her kneel at my feet. The smell of love filled the world. I could not resist. I ran to my room, and again the monster dominated me" (231).[9]

At the same time, the unrealized desire for power is displaced to writing.[10] When he is writing, the narrator pictures himself strong, in charge of his destiny (64), attempting, in the imaginary space, to satisfy his original lack. Despite proposing to tell the truth, what *Eurídice* ultimately does is expose the open scar, the opposite of the truth. In this line of interpretation, the commentary made by the taciturn fellow prisoner gains importance, when he says that the truth "was almost never what we anticipated to be the truth. What we expected to be our truth cannot be more than an effort of our lies, of simulation, of strength forged by our senses or by our will" (126).[11]

The novel, which had proposed to expose the truth, ends by revealing its simulation, exposing Julinho's fragility. And the writing not only provides him "the certainty that the only reason for my failure came from Tijuca street" (260)—thus contradicting what he himself had affirmed previously—but also shows him that he cannot satisfy the maxim told him by Campos, an elderly resident of the Catete boarding house: "Since you are in the line of fire, you must be a man. Strength, son, lots of strength, or you will become a banana. Women are serious business, son" (277).

III

This reading of *Eurídice* unveils the psychoanalytical substratum that is interwoven in several of José Lins do Rego's characters, and it is possible to undertake a broader reading that includes this 1947 text, *Menino de engenho* and the rest of the sugarcane cycle, *Fogo morto,* and the autobiography, *Meus verdes anos.* In *Eurídice* the violence of the Brazilian social formation, latent in the texts dealing with the world of sugar plantations, is explicit, offering an escape valve that had not been adequately formulated by the personages of *Fogo morto,* who were characterized by impotence. Now, the domination is manifested in the male/female relationship (another version of the hierarchical structure of power that marks Brazilian society), in the necessity of the impotent character, representing the declining patriarchal order, physically to subject the "fragile" sex that escapes his control in an urban space undergoing a process of transformation, where the weakened control of the master is not enough to tame the feminine other. In this sense, the examination of *Eurídice* helps compose a panel that was outlined with a discussion of the rural novels, and it shows how much the traditional, agrarian order left marks on the urban society that was being formed.

The dissolution of the nuclear family undermines the protagonists (such as Carlos de Melo or Julinho) as individuals, and the decadence of the patriarchal and masculine order generates weak and impotent men, authentic "bananas." The male characters, weakened in the social sphere, having generally entered into contact with the urban world, attempt to recover a form of power in the sexual field, through machismo. Sexuality is thus confused with the anxiety of dominating women. The good times were those of Colonel José Paulino (a time when men possessed their female slaves at will), and such men were true almond trees with their roots deep in the ground.

The sugarcane cycle narrates things past: there, it is not the power of one family that was extinguished; rather, the way this domination was organized has become anachronistic (Süssekind, *Tal Brasil, qual romance?* 165).[12] The colonelistic system is not put in check; José Paulino ends up safe and sound. In José Lins do Rego's fiction I do not find a "critical vision of the socio-economic structure described" (Dacanal), but rather a nostalgia for the traditional order of the plantation mansion, not yet swallowed by the refinery, which impedes a questioning position in relation to the narrated world. The decline of this rural universe leaves the characters without the strength to act and transform the reality around them, or even to outline an efficient attempt at understanding the present that surrounds them. In this sense, the novel's title also refers to the characters, who are metaphorically marked by the fogo morto.

As the fictitious memorialist Graciliano Ramos says in *Em liberdade,* "the decadence of the present does not come from the past; it is exclusively fruit of the incompetence of today's men" (Santiago, 118). The generation of Carlos or Julinho or even, as we are inclined to believe, José Lins do Rego himself, were unable to reproduce the strong patriarch, the virile he-men who mounted slave women, incapable of grasping the patriarchal rod with the same manliness as the old Colonel José Paulino. These weak creatures, as novelists or pseudo-authors, are left with restoring the past in the imaginary space of literary representation, where they narrate their trajectory of impotence and how the leafy almond trees gave fruit to broken and failed bananas.

The Narrow Limits —A Reading of Graciliano Ramos's *Memórias do Cárcere*

> No one enjoys complete freedom; we begin oppressed by syntax and end up in the office of political and social order, but within the narrow limits to which grammar and the law confine us, we can still move around.
>
> —*Graciliano Ramos*

In *Memórias do cárcere,*[1] Graciliano Ramos (the subject of the écriture) constantly attempts to interpret what had happened to him. All of the events of his imprisonment appear as signs of a discourse that he, the interpreter, attempts to read. The various questions that dot especially the beginning of the memoirs reveal his anxiousness to decodify what is occurring and to verify the correctness of his reading. He later transfers his efforts of interpretation to other characters, whether representatives of order, such as Captain Lobo, or prisoners, like Gaúcho or the homosexual kitchen worker.

Graciliano was incarcerated for a period of ten months (March 1936 to January 1937).[2] *Memórias do cárcere* was written ten years later and published posthumously (1953), "as is fitting for a book of memoirs" (1:8). It narrates Graciliano's arrest in Maceió and his later transfer to Rio de Janeiro, his confinement in a cell, the days spent in the Ilha Grande prison, and the less-confining situation in the penal ward for first offenders.

The writer undertakes this "descent into hell" armed with a set of preconceived notions deriving from his situation as a bourgeois intellectual, replete with such values as dignity, on the one hand, and the logic of meaning, on the other. The Estado Novo dictatorship's repressive apparatus offers him, in turn, another set of references, and it is easy to deduce that, because of their lack of confluence, there will occur a painful collision between the two.

The authorities do not explain to Graciliano why he has been arrested or what his supposed crimes were. There is no interrogation, no witnesses, no trial, no accusation, no formal procedure that would indicate at least a simulacrum of justice. They never say where they are taking him. This lack of explanations and the resulting instability—the inability to certify if his interpretation of the experience he is undergoing is correct—do not merely produce the sensation of being the victim of injustice but are also fundamental for the process of degradation and moral violence to which the dictatorship subjects individuals. Graciliano expects a "major condemnation," although he feels he is being treated unjustly, since he is not a communist in either ideological terms or in terms of party affiliation. Instead, they offer him a suppression of the limits of what he judges to be human dignity, a lack of meaning, or, if you will, an unsuspected meaning within the petit-bourgeois contours that seem to serve as his frame of reference.

The Estado Novo was characterized by an extreme centralization, reflected, for example, in state intervention in agricultural production (by means of various institutes, such as those of coffee and sugar), in the organization and administration of the economy (the Volta Redonda steel mill and the creation of diverse consultative organs), in the containment of the working class demands (through labor legislation and the Ministry of Labor), and in the control and "filtering" of the circulation of information through censorship (the creation of DIP). At the same time, Vargas made political alliances with diverse ruling segments and violently repressed any genuinely popular dissidence (e.g., the actions of Filinto Müller as head of the federal police). This meant silencing the spurious voices that could stain the Estado Novo's ideological project, which seemed to pursue what one might call absolute "purism." Thus, in *Memórias do cárcere,* one perceives an accentuated movement toward uniformity by those who represent this extremely authoritarian project. Paradoxically, however, this leveling provokes the emergence of other differences, as we will shortly see.

The legal order, created by the state apparatus, necessarily requires univocality. The letter of the law has to impede polysemy, stopping the flow of interpretations, which tends to be infinite. Jurisprudence and legislative codes need monosignification, thus stifling the pluralist activity characteristic of interpretive practice. The less ambiguous, the better the legal norm. In this sense, the law operates as a sort of "author-function," as Foucault defines it, interrupting the vertiginous dissemination of attributions of meaning.[3] In the same sense, the subject gives meaning to the world, and it is constituted by a limitless number of interpretations, by a broad spectrum of texts. The play of signification thus also passes through the subject who, by interpreting the world, tends to interrupt the proliferation of versions, acting as an "author-function."

In this conflict between the law and the pluralistic nature of interpretive practice, we have an outline of the conflict between the individual and the State. To the extent that social and historical reality offer themselves to interpretation as text, alongside the law is one "author-function," and alongside the subject is another "author-function." In *Memórias do cárcere,* the two poles are in conflict in the exact proportion to which we have an authoritarian regime and an intellectual who opposes it and is incarcerated by it.

More importantly, Graciliano as interpreter lacks the notion that the dictatorship presents itself to him discursively. The problematics of language would only become a burning issue in the humanities after his death in 1953. But the situation delineated above underwent notable changes, since it is Graciliano who comes armed with a logical and preconceived predisposition based on concepts of a moral order. If it is characteristic of the law to be inflexible, his expectation is that the agents who represent it will behave accordingly. However, both in the specific universe of *Memórias* and in Brazilian society in general, the law is ambiguous and contradictory.[4] The basic concern of the repressive apparatus is precisely to eliminate the characteristics that permit difference, mixing political prisoners and thieves, treating men like animals and in total promiscuity in the dungeons of the human condition.

The process of degradation can be followed throughout the four volumes. Near the beginning, the narrator-personage perceives that his "silly petit bourgeois prerogatives would end" (1:26). His contact with the subworld of the prison creates "calluses on the soul." In the cells there is no door or curtain in the latrine, thus vilifying its visitors. A powerful black man puts a pistol barrel against the author's chest just to scare him when he arrives on the ship that will take him to Rio. He refers to the hold of the Manaus as a "descent into hell": filthy puddles of urine, a nauseating pool, and a new socialization among prisoners (visible in the commerce that is established) soon show Graciliano "unknown aspects of society" (1:161) which he had not previously experienced: "We need to live in hell, submerge in the social underground, in order to evaluate actions that we would be unable to understand in the world here above" (1:166).

It is worth noting how Graciliano thinks in terms of binary oppositions (a tendency of Western thought): the "high" is good and is marked positively; the "low" is bad, seen as negative. Since he writes "here above," I deduce that, at the moment of writing (ten years after his imprisonment), he is "above," reinstated in his social situation and in his environment, and thus differentiated from those "there below." Later, he repeats the "high" versus "low" relationship, and he speaks of "outside" versus "inside," "normal behavior" versus "abnormal behavior," etc. As Antelo puts it, "Forced to decide between two terms, Graciliano's rigid dialectic values one of the two poles" (54). The effort to interpret what has occurred continues at the moment of telling, a decade removed from the lived experience, as if the interpreter were still searching for a way to decipher the Estado Novo oracle in his memoirs.

The height of degradation and lack of understanding occurs in the Correctional Facility. When one prisoner is beaten, all the others stay with their arms crossed, passive, including—to his own astonishment—Graciliano himself: "We were tatters; we were dry wells; we were disgraced egos filled with fear. They had reduced us to that" (3:77). The potash put in the beans causes colic and gas, destroying the detainees' intestines. Graciliano needs to urinate, and he has to do so in the open holes in the floor where prisoners defecate. They do not have, the narrator notes, a minimal level of dignity.

When they arrive, a soldier explicitly stresses the elimination of any distinctive features: "Here there are no rights. Listen to me. No rights at all. Whoever was important outside can forget it. Here none of you are important. You are all the same. Those who have protectors don't come in here. Attention. You did not come here for rehabilitation. You came here to die" (3:80). The soldier's threat is revealing as to the selection undertaken by the Estado Novo, attempting to "purify" the regime: those who supposedly dissent and those who do not have protectors are excluded; those who do enjoy protection must collaborate with authoritarianism to save their own skins and avoid being sent to the dictatorship's dungeons.

The "barbed-wire corral" is, in short, a place where men are leveled downward. Erasing the marks which, according to a logical and predictable scheme, distinguish people from each other, the two poles mix together. Cubano, a prisoner in charge of the others' lineup, wants to force Graciliano to eat, because his health is deteriorating, and fights with him. The narrator comments, "an unusual, rather odd person": "even to reveal feelings of generosity, brutality was indispensable in him" (3:182). The encounter with a homosexual bothers Graciliano, causing a nausea mixed with gratitude: *"The existence of a heart in such abnormalities had never occurred to me; distant, exclusivistic and rigid, I had become used to judging them as merely sordid"* (3:129; emphasis added). The episode involving this "strange individual" shows him that "there was something very pure in his nauseating depravity." "Exclusivistic and rigid," Graciliano had labeled homosexuality as "depraved," unable to see something "pure" in it. Again, the binary perspective, which represses and excludes differences by privileging one pole and suppressing the other. With the leveling occasioned by prison, the "abnormalities" are revealed, the peculiarities reestablished, provoking amazement in the narrator, accustomed to a binary logic and once incapable of supposing the existence of a heart in sordidness or generosity in brutishness.

Language is also affected by this degradation that lowers everything and everyone: "In that environment, the vocabulary of the hustlers and the militants of illegal political organizations mixed together; little by little this chaotic agglomeration invaded common language" (3:119). Graciliano is recognized as a notable stylist who submits language to a sort of dissection, stripping the sentence to its skeleton as if removing fat and excess. Although he admits the popular and the regional in his writing, Tristão de Athayde has called his diction "classical."[5] Perhaps this classicist perspective was, in reality, a reaction against contagion and impurity. His comments concerning the impure dialects of prison's invasion of "common language" at the very least raise this suspicion.

In short, armed with a binary logic to read the subworld of the prison, the interpreter Graciliano cannot account for its meaning, because the boundaries that permit differentiation between common language and the jargon of hustlers and/or political militants, the sordid and the pure, civility/composure and promiscuity, compassion and insensitivity, and generosity and brutality are purposely dissolved and confused. His reading fails as much for being based on a repertoire of moral references incompatible with the reality of repression (what totalitarian regime respects human rights?), culminating in the "breakdown of high values" (again the "high"), as for its insistence on searching for order (if one is a homosexual or a crook one cannot be generous) where ambiguity and contradictions rule. Ironically, by attempting to understand the Estado Novo's discourse as logical, grounded in the presupposition that authoritarianism has to be semantically univocal, the one who runs the risk of being authoritarian is, at least on the level of interpretation, Graciliano himself.

The Estado Novo's strategy consisted in erasing rigid differences by eliminating nuances and searching for a leveling uniformity. At the end of this undertaking, however, the result, according to its logical framework, seems to make it possible for the figures to change sides (e.g., the sordid becomes generous), thus subverting the protagonist's expectations. Consequently, intepretations of Tupinambá fascism undertaken by the interpreter Graciliano are not successful.

One of the first examples of the Estado Novo's action in *Memórias do cárcere* occurs in the passage in which the narrator, going against explicit instructions, enters the sergeant's bathroom because that of the officers was occupied. Captain Lobo calls it a serious infraction. They hold him responsible and exaggerate the incident; all attempts at defense are useless (1:83). Prison's logic is different: one cannot disobey what has been determined nor try to defend oneself. The deeper one descends into the prison subworld, the more tenuous the rules become. The law is no longer fixed and congealed, blocking the flow of interpretations. Rather, it acquires a mobile profile, indifferent to univocality—it is capricious, subject to error, interests, and passions (1:98). It also becomes a law disseminated in the vertigo of discourse instead of being immobile, which makes it more difficult to grasp than if it were solidified in the stone texts of exceptional acts.

Graciliano comes from a patriarchal social group, characterized by hierarchy and traversed by contradictions.[6] Prison suspends the law in the name of the law, which becomes sinuous and slippery to the narrator-interpreter, who does not understand what is happening. Dictatorship, the extreme consummation of order, which should function as an interruption of interpretations, reveals itself to be "without limits" in the confines of the prison cells, bringing about a plurisignification instead of a semantic monovalence.

Authorities ask him to open the letter he received, but they say it is a mere formality. Graciliano's astonishment: "Odd. It was really taking the routine very far to force a person to do something and then say it had no value, that it was a useless order" (1:100). It is precisely a case of establishing a lack of meaning and the inviability of codification.

Captain Lobo, who had been irritated by the bathroom episode, offers Graciliano a loan when he is to be transferred to Rio de Janeiro. In his recollection of the offer, the narrator's discomfort is evident:

> Captain Lobo, therefore, was *going against the norm.* In a certain sense the case was a sort of desertion. *Impossible to explain.* If he condemned my ideas, without really knowing them, why did he offer me that *incoherent* support [. . .]. We accept a certain number of principles, we judge them to be *firm, then we suddenly notice a gap in them*—and things do not occur as we had foreseen: they occur in just the opposite way. *The exception bothers us and we have to reformulate our opinions* [. . .]. *It was difficult to conceive* of someone who would give of himself voluntarily to benefit an adversary. This renunciation of propriety dizzied me. (1:112–13; emphasis added)

No reason is offered for Graciliano's transfer to the south. It would be more reasonable, from his perspective, for him to dig wells or teach children to read there in the northeast. The lack of coherence and meaning exasperates him: there is no explicit motive for anything, reasons for actions are unknown; initiative is taken from the detainees, and the most guarded desires and feelings are subject to examination. Prisoners are forced to obey unreasonable procedures, and a series of questions goes without answer, with no possibility of verification (1:193). To maintain insensitivity in force, prisoners are moved frequently so they do not create solid bonds. The strangeness and the lack of understanding of events take control of *Memórias do cárcere*'s narrator.

Another facet of repression is the preservation of appearances. Searches are done hurriedly to fulfill an obligation. The police apparatus ultimately lacks the rigor that the prisoners had supposed "on the outside." Individuals are always ready "to simulate lack of attention, to doze at the precise moment, if such slip-ups do not violate the letter of the regulation," which is not taken literally (2:234). This "irregular" attitude on the part of the police—they are mechanical and punctual in the obedience of the manual, but in difficult moments they themselves suggest unacceptable behavior—also surprises Graciliano. His great lesson is this: the coexistence of opposites. There is purity in abjection, grandeur in misery. According to the values of his class, opposites are hierarchically separated. When limits are annulled in prison, the poles scandalously coexist. There is purity and grandeur both on the part of those responsible for order (soldiers, guards, jailers) and on the part of those punished by order (the prisoners). Gaúcho and Paulo Turco are capable of worthy actions which are incomprehensible to Graciliano. The prison experience gave Graciliano a more complex view of human beings.

In the dictatorship's backrooms, however, the desire for order is satisfied by appearances while it attempts to erase each and every sense or possibility of testing the attributions of meaning. Prohibitions are loosened and exist as if to be violated. The law is not the law. One of the problems of authoritarian practice, of violence in Brazil, resides in simulation. It does not always declare itself manifestly and openly. A slippery ambiguity coexists with the monolithic package of censorship, repression, and exceptional acts. Consequently, the surface, the mask, and the disguise are what matter. In *Memórias do cárcere,* refuting the protagonist's presuppositions, authoritarianism is inscribed precisely at this level—in the sphere of representation, in the duplicity that the term permits.

> This case suggested to me an opinion, perhaps false, about military discipline which I still hold today. In it I suspect that rigor is superficial. Indispensable are the shoes shined bright with

> shagreen and oil, clean collars, all buttons fastened, straight and upright backs. Right legs should move simultaneously, then left legs, and no finger should be out of line in a salute. It is necessary to look twenty steps ahead, and all steps, in accordance with the march's rhythm, must have the same number of centimeters. Of course there are other duties as well, but of the same sort, leading toward the recruit's mechanization. Once certain formulas are memorized and indispensable movements learned, the soldier can forget obligations and even the principles learned in civilian life. The important thing is an impeccable appearance. (1:64)

This, consequently, is the legacy prison left Graciliano Ramos. Despite the harsh treatment and the horrible experience, he in fact enjoyed certain privileges, particularly if we compare him with other detainees. The episode involving the infraction of Captain Lobo's order to use the officer's bathroom illustrates the distinction with which Graciliano and other political prisoners are contemplated, especially in the Pavilhão dos Primários. When he returns to it, he learns the importance of the cost of food and comments that a tenth of the amount spent to maintain a man in the Pavilhão was not spent to feed nine hundred prisoners in the Correctional Facility (4:27).

In fact, the time spent in the Correctional Facility is the worst moment of prison, where social divisions are most diffuse. Graciliano lives through the dulling of the "prudery of conscience" and the change in moral values which take away his means of being dignified (see the episode concerning the priest's visit, 3:171).

The narrator seems to attribute an "essential nature" to the social situation of individuals: "Evidently people are not distinguished by belonging to one class or another; their position is what gives them the appearance of inferiority or superiority. Evidently. But why evidently? Observation told me just the opposite. A man from the sticks, used to seeing dirty, starving, humble, animal-like half-breeds, was forced involuntarily to suppose an *essential difference* between them and the bosses. Material facts opposed the ideal—and this displeased me" (2:66; emphasis added).

If I read the passage correctly, it explains the stock of references Graciliano uses to interpret the prison subworld as well as his attitude toward the law, and it helps to understand his efforts to regain his distinctive characteristics. Graciliano is unable to comprehend that meaning does not exist in presence, that it is always deferred, depending therefore on the position—in this case, that which the individual occupies in the social structure—and on the dialogical relationship that one might establish between what is being interpreted and other terms deriving from other texts and discourses. The social being's meaning thus depends on his/her interaction with others, and never on an "essential," predetermined plenitude, as Graciliano seems to believe.

Graciliano's attempt to repossess the emblems of his class begins to be delineated clearly in the episode concerning the bed he bought from Gaúcho, which another prisoner had wanted. Earlier, Graciliano had said that "I am not bourgeois, I do not exploit anyone" (3:118); but now his bourgeois nature flourishes in an outburst of anger, and he yells at the obtruder: "I am an owner" (3:146–47). Leaving aside the detail that he calls some personages "negroes," he dislikes the fact that he has to mix with "thieves, bums, hustlers, the dregs of slums, who are reduced to picking up cigarette butts off the ground" (3:105), thus annulling an "essential difference." I deduce that the leveling bothers him because, in other circumstances—outside of prison, "here above"—thieves, bums, hustlers, and the dregs of slums would be at one extreme and would not coexist with a bourgeois intellectual, situated at the other extreme. Reinforcing the argument, I might point out that the narrator rejects the proximity of Pai João, a little, "simian" black ("doesn't he know that I don't like such intimacy?"; "I don't like this. It's better for us to live apart" [4:99]).[7]

On leaving the hell of the Correctional Facility, Graciliano is imbued with the desire to "retrieve the personality that had been diluted in an abject environment" (3:192). In consonance with my interpretation, where one reads "personality," one should understand the symbols that indicate privileges and social nuances. Graciliano obstinately attempts to reconstitute them when he arrives back at the Pavilhão, where he will be treated with a certain deference (outside, important friends are working for his release). He obtains a piece of wood, and with it and a piece of string he fashions a sort of coat hanger where he hangs his rumpled coat and trousers; he brushes the clothes before hanging them, has the white pieces washed, and cleans his shoes, giving them a reasonable appearance (4:16).

We should remember further that the narrator writes, at a certain moment, that the poor treatment and the "mysterious suicides" apply to prisoners "more or less involved in the revolt of 1935." And to the question "What the hell do I have to do with them?" he answers, "Certainly they would not stick me with needles nor make me jump from a high window." He is thus calm at the beginning, since he does not remember "having uttered a syllable that would offend authority" (1:90). The problem is not that there is torture, but that he not be tortured; not that there is arbitrary rule, but that the arbitrary rule not turn against him. Besides being a poor reader of the Estado Novo, Graciliano Ramos wants to remain free of the "narrow limits" established by the dictatorship.

In April 1941, four years after having been freed from the Correctional Facility, Graciliano begins collaborating with the journal *Cultura Política,* published by the Departamento de Imprensa e Propaganda (Antelo, 27). It is important to note that the novelist, between 1938 and 1945, has much to do with the Estado Novo (Facioli, 76): "Because of its extension, duration, and signification, Graciliano's collaboration with the Estado Novo's press can hardly be explained by the mere difficulty of survival, as the version which has tended to become 'official' would have it" (Facioli, 65).

* * *

It is perhaps unnecessary to note that what was written above does not intend to criticize Graciliano Ramos—it is impossible to know how each of us would behave if we underwent such an atrocious experience. I have attempted to show, rather, the contradictions that pervade *Memórias do cárcere* in an analysis that hopes to contribute to a better understanding of his production.[8]

Above all, I have been interested in emphasizing the "mistaken" reading that the narrator undertakes of the marks of authoritarianism. In the context of totalitarian regimes, how does one interpret the social game? How does one read the painful inscriptions of the discourse of power?

The four volumes of Graciliano's prison memoirs raise such questions. The protagonist bases his narrative on reflections supported by binary oppositions and moral values. Dictatorships, however, do not respect human dignity, and, at least in the Brazilian case and in the work at hand, they do not always manifest themselves in a clear and sensible manner: questions concerning meaning and the possibility of verifying the correctness of interpretations are raised, and a lack of sense comes to the surface. With this, there exists a considerable dosage of the absurd in authoritarianism. The Estado Novo's project, as seen in *Memórias do cárcere,* seems to consist, in consonance with the centralization that characterizes it in the political sphere, in equalizing, making uniform, leveling, and eliding the social symbols that distinguish individuals. Paradoxically, in the underground of the pavilions and of the Ilha Grande, such neutralization in search of univocality ultimately provokes the emergence of other differences, which confuse the efforts of comprehension of the interpreter Graciliano, since in the people, gestures, and episodes that pass before his reading are interwoven sordidness with grandeur, causing a short circuit in the rigid schemes of decodification. At the same time, an ambiguity appears in the law, which is presented as dubious, skittish, coinciding with the false rigor and the simulation of intolerance, disarming the protagonist-narrator's crystallized preconceptions and logic of meaning.

The orthodox dogmatism of Graciliano's readings, which tend not to reserve space for ambivalence, lacks a certain astuteness, an understanding of the other, an acceptance of difference, of the dissemination of meaning, of the logic of supplementarity. Without this shifting, slippery, and vertiginous conception of signification, his interpretations risk the danger of being just as authoritarian as the fascism that he certainly intended to denounce.[9] We should, perhaps, adopt a more clever position so we can move between the narrow limits imposed by grammar and law, always transgressing all forms of power.

The Pearl Necklace —Notes for the Study of the Brazilian Urban Novel in the 1930s

> For this very reason the necklace will never be recomposed. The beads are together now, but always fragmentarily, attempting to reconstitute of that which has no solution.
>
> —*Galeão Coutinho*

I

In an essay about literature during the Old Republic, Alfredo Bosi calls attention to the irrational, primitivistic, and mythifying contours—the search for an eternal present—of Brazilian modernism of the 1920s. According to him, 1930 will offer a "historical and concrete," "contradictory" portrait of Brazil, "the object of a new realism and a political literature" ("As letras na Primeira República," 315–16). Bosi's assertion makes critics with a social orientation turn their attention toward the literary production of the second modernist moment, since the "heroic phase," having generated a mythical portrait of Brazilian reality, was not successful in capturing the tensions caused by the country's modernization. To a great extent, the importance of this moment derives from its attempt to interpret the *transition* Brazilian society was undergoing, narrated by the period's novel, which relates the decadence of the seignorial class.

In this chapter I propose to explore one of the still little-understood veins of the period's literature, the urban novel, represented by authors such as Dyonelio Machado (*Os ratos*), Rosário Fusco (*O agressor*), Amando Fontes (*Os Corumbas*, *Rua do Siriri*), João

Alphonsus (*Totônio Pacheco*), and Galeão Coutinho (*Memórias de Simão, o caolho, Confidências de Dona Marcolina, A vocação de Vitorino Lapa, Vovô Morungaba*). I will limit my discussion to three narratives by Galeão Coutinho, also with the purpose of placing his name in circulation again, since he was so widely read in his time and has today fallen into unjust oblivion.

II

The novels *Memórias de Simão, o caolho* (1937) and *Vovô Morungaba* (1938) were published initially in the press, avidly consumed, and reached multiple editions in the year of their publication (*Memórias*, 8). The first seems to be Coutinho's most respected text, and in it we find the two basic ingredients of his fiction: humor and a "bitter aftertaste" (Mário da Silva Brito)—a certain skepticism, much like that of Machado de Assis, toward the human condition.[1]

The novel is narrated by the protagonist Simão and undertakes a radiograph of São Paulo's middle class in the 1930s as well as of conjugal life. Simão is extremely machista: women are occupied by "frivolity and odd-jobs" and men by great ideas. Returning home like a "new Columbus," Simão, an inveterate womanizer, coexists with the "microcosm" of his wife, Dona Marcolina. What he is unable to understand is that she is the one who holds power in the domestic sphere. Simão sees her much more as a housewife and mother and feels supported and protected when she pampers him during an illness.[2]

Completely dissatisfied between the four walls of his home, Simão searches for refuge in the street. When he becomes Maria Otília's lover, he reencounters peace and power, since she is docile and submissive, "a timid little bird blown by a storm": "Not at all cerebral, all instinct, she just wants peace between four walls, a poor, passive animal, with no violent desires or crazy dreams, ready to obey, seeing in the man an all-powerful being whose will nothing in this world can resist" (240).

My interpretation of this novel and its judgment of the timid Paulista middle class and husband-wife relations centers on the Simão–Marcolina–Maria Otília triangle. I suggest that it suffers the consequences of the patriarchal legacy, showing the marks the traditional order had left in the urban context. Married life is seen as a power struggle between the man and the woman. The man's power is weakened, and the emergence of the feminine problematic is thematized in its birth.[3] All of this takes place in an urban space, on whose shoulders weighs the past, still not totally dissipated, of a rural society whose values "had been displaced untouched to the city" (Muricy, 55). The subsequent reading of other texts by Galeão Coutinho confirms this initial hypothesis.

I first read *Confidências de Dona Marcolina* (1949) with extreme curiosity. In it I expected the counterpoint of Simão's machista discourse, the perspective of his better half—if not a feminine perspective, at least one opposed to that of the narrator-protagonist of the 1937 novel. The two versions, if contrastive, would constitute a mark of originality in Brazilian literature.[4]

The dialogue between the two texts in fact occurs. The narrator of the 1949 novel, however, is not Simão's wife, but rather Justino, a friend of the couple who has known Simão for many years. Dona Marcolina does not represent the woman's voice, and the title falsifies the narrative's scope, since we do not truly have the "confessions" of a middle-class woman of the 1930s/1940s. Because even Dona Marcolina's stories are checked by Justino at a table in a bar with his old friend, thus casting doubt on her testimony.

An incurable macho, Simão ends up repeating Padre Gregório's sentence: "A woman is like a child and a black man: she lies and steals" (122). Prejudice aside, his preconceived idea about the opposite sex, clear in so many examples ("the more ignorant the woman is, the more of a woman she is" [54]), barely hides the play of power that unfolds between men and women. Simão prefers dumb women, like Maria Otília in *Memórias,* because they are more docile and easier to dominate: "I would only like a woman who is 'free and disencumbered of any responsibility.' A type that I know well: a simple little woman, with no airs of literature, society, and modernism" (108); "we like maids because they are a kind of slave. It makes us feel good and powerful to support and protect them, which is the same as saying to love them" (109).

The passages are evident and speak for themselves: would it be necessary here to recall the seignorial scene, the master's sons maintaining sexual relations with slaves and maids, with the puritan island of the home preserved for spiritual and sacred love?[5] Love, for Simão, is synonymous with subjugating the woman.

Dona Marcolina, in turn, also holds a wealth of clichés about men: "a house without a man is in danger" and "a man is a man" (21) exemplify her attitude, as if implicitly recognizing (although bothered by it) the man's right to commit adultery—"we don't trust men even when they dress like angels" (197). For her, the blame belongs to "meddling women": "a woman doesn't like ticks only because she doesn't know which one is the male" (23).

The narrator Justino is equally machista: for him women are incapable of being logical or of having an awareness of time, "revolving in a narrow world" (49), exchanging among themselves "the small change of their small ideas" (232): "the thousands of domestic worries, occupying all their facilities, disputes with the grocer, arguments with the maid, disagreements with their husbands because of a cigarette butt on the floor, or—more seriously—to discover where he got the strand of long, blond hair found on his lapel, all of these things retard the mental progress of thousands, millions of housewives" (38–39).

Justino is omniscient on numerous occasions, and he interweaves the narration with his own commentaries. The way to minimize his omniscience resides in "doubts" or in checking with Simão about the information obtained from Dona Marcolina, "in order to clarify controversial points" or to correct omissions in his confidante's statements. His attitude of verifying her version with his friend is so frequent that the narrator even asks about the propriety of the novel's title: "In the final analysis, who is talking? That is the question the reader has the right to ask [. . .]. Are these the 'confessions of Dona Marcolina' or a pretext for her husband to continue his slanderous *Memórias*?" (124).

In another essay, *A permanência do círculo,* I attempted to show how nineteenth-century Brazilian fiction is enclosed in the narrow circle of the dominant classes, expressing seignorial and patriarchal values. This structure perseveres in the novel of the 1930s, although the values are more fragile and the rural world is in clear decay. The expectation that the *Confidências* would initiate a counterpoint to the *Memórias* disappears with an examination of the three main characters: far from constituting discrepant and contrastive voices, Simão, the narrator Justino, and even Marcolina, in the final analysis, share the same prejudiced, masculine focus detected in a whole tradition of the Brazilian novel. In this text we thus do not have a discourse of *difference* (in this case, a feminine discourse) but rather the voice of the *same.*

The extent to which Simão and Dona Marcolina's adventures, in São Paulo of the 1930s, are indebted to the rural heritage is condensed in the metaphor of the *pearl necklace:* Dona Marcolina's friends are, like her, from Sorocaba. The old "necklace was broken and the pearls scattered throughout the city of São Paulo" (17). Their habit of visiting each other (an old custom of small rural towns) is a frustrated attempt to recompose the necklace. The topic of conversation during their visits is always "the good old days," which have changed so much in the large city. Marcolina's birthday party (144 ff.) clearly reveals the true difference between the young people and those who are over 50, raised on rural fazendas and repressed by a feudal education. This passage—this transformation—from the rural to the urban becomes clear in *Vovô Morungaba,* the piece that is lacking to confirm the reading I have undertaken of one-eyed Simão's memoirs, with its nostalgic pathos.

* * *

In the preface to *Vovô Morungaba* (1938), Genolino Amado writes that Galeão Coutinho's literary production focuses on "the suffering of anonymous people, who have fallen from the small middle class, but who have not yet become proletarians, and who struggle against marginalization in the ocean of large cities" (11). The novel's relevance resides in this reencounter of fiction with the city, abandoning the social environment that had previously nourished it.

Contradictorily, Amado continues, the Brazilian novelist had distanced himself from the city just as the city was expanding and providing novelistic subjects, thus interrupting a tradition that runs through Manuel Antônio de Almeida, Macedo, the urban Alencar, all of Machado, Pompéia, much of Aluísio Azevedo, and some Taunay. Literature responds to the growth of Rio de Janeiro only with Lima Barreto, whose work is set in the suburbs instead of the metropolis as such. The novelists ignored, in their books, the country's capital, at that time with two million inhabitants.

The new authors wrote about sugarcane fields, rural areas, small backland towns, and fishing villages, although they themselves lived in Rio de Janeiro. Those who were in the big city in literary terms wrote intimist works more interested in the mysteries of the soul than in external existence and the street. And Amado regrets that the whole range of manifestations of the process of urbanization—to which Machado de Assis's myopic and tired eyes were attentive in a much smaller Rio—did not fascinate writers.

For Amado, the reflourishing of literature emphasizing rural Brazil did not represent a bucolic evasion, but rather a stance that corresponded to a new social conscience. With Modernism, in the full political effervescence of the 1930s, novelists became absorbed with problems of the interior, denouncing the true face of the inequality and cruelty of the Brazilian rural world, Amado concludes, calling attention to the novelists' neglect of the urban universe (Amado, 12, 13). Even the most recent criticism seems to insist on the mistake of privileging the regionalist tendency to the detriment of the narrative prose that seems to propose to capture the country's urban expansion. Writers such as Dyonelio Machado, Amando Fontes (who idealizes the working class in *Os Corumbas* and prostitutes in *Rua do Siriri*), or Marques Rebelo (*Marafa, A estrela sobe*) constitute this vein, which flows today in the literature of Rubem Fonseca, Dalton Trevisan, João Antônio, and João Gilberto Noll, among others.

Barra Mansa and Mata-sete are the main characters of *Vovô Morungaba.* Barra is a civil servant with a modest income which barely permits him to support his family and pay his debts. Thus he lives on borrowed cash, attempting to avoid his creditors. He is a "rolling stone" (24) whose irreducible fatalism is summarized in the "it's not worth the effort" (53) which expresses his inertia and impotence: "Barra is a loser, as they say. For him, it makes no difference if rivers run uphill or down" (56). Barra Mansa always relies on his companion, who is quicker to invent alternative ways to get money: "Without *Mata-sete* he was like a headless body. He always thought through his friend's head" (86).

In this sense, Barra Mansa reduplicates, in the urban context, equally impotent characters who appear in regionalist novels, such as Carlos in *Bangüê* or Mestre Zé Amaro and Colonel Lula de Holanda in *Fogo Morto,* both by José Lins do Rego. Or, if one prefers, he is a relative of the Belo Horizonte scribe Belmiro Borba of Cyro dos Anjos's *O amanuense Belmiro,* with whom he shares the profession of civil servant.

Barra Mansa never feels responsible for his problems, nor does he have an awareness of the unjust society in which he lives. The explanation is either that he is "unfavored," with evil spirits against him, or his grandfather, the old Morungaba, is the cause of his misery. Like the protagonist of *O amanuense Belmiro,* Barra Mansa comes from a rural background, which is inscribed even in his nickname.[6]

The São Paulo that serves as a setting for Barra Mansa's misadventures is in a full process of modernization. The manual "Compendium of the Perfect Salesman," "a true catechism in the art of salesmanship," teaches how to palm off refrigerators, automobiles, radios, electric waxers, washing machines, vacuum cleaners, and other household appliances, indicating a fever of consumerism and incipient automation.

The same devastating march of modern times destroys the old Morungaba's coffee mill. The passage in which Barra converses with him in his imagination mixes a nostalgic tone with references to the fact that his grandfather, unlike the impotent and apathetic grandson, was a decisive man and the epicenter of the fazenda, which succumbed to modernization at the hands of someone from the city, distant from the countryside.

> He saw his native scenarios, his grandfather's coffee mill, moved by the water wheel, on the edge of the hill from which the unhappy Honorato's Fazenda Velha looked out over the valley with the empty sockets of its large, open windows. The big wheel turned slowly under the weight of the water from the pond; and, thanks to the admirable play of axles, bearings, and pulleys, the mill filled the air with its infernal noise. Barra would go there with his grandfather, and it was a pleasure to watch the coffee beans' martyrdom in the hulling machines, pulping mills, and separators, going up and down in the buckets and coming out clean and lead-colored in a wooden tube. After being weighed and sewed, the bags were transported on the backs of black men to the warehouse and from there sent to Barra Mansa's station. *All because of Vovô Morungaba.* When there was a problem, the workers would call the old man, who, using pincers, drills, screwdrivers, files, augers, hammers, saws, and chisels, would quickly fix the machine. Later, Seu Antero, *a modern fazendeiro who never left Rio de Janeiro,* built a steam mill with hulling machines and separators, all in the latest model, and Vovô Mo-

> rungaba's mill began losing its clientele and went under, sold like scrap iron. (178; emphasis added)[7]

The decadence of the past, in the novel, is coagulated in two micronarratives: that of crazy Rosa (one of the richest landowners of the city, who falls into poverty with Abolition [167]) and that of Colonel Honorato, "who wore only white and rode only a white horse" and who "built an entirely white house in the city," besides not letting blacks put their feet even on his veranda (he was also ruined by Abolition [168–69]). Instead of going crazy, he loses his speech due to "the cruel misfortunes of fate" (169).

Little by little, reminiscences begin taking control of Barra, who feels himself more and more attracted by his past: "where did all of this go!" (117); "how long ago was all of that?" (170). In contrast to Barra Mansa, his grandfather was, as already noted, a man of action. Similar to an old tree rooted in the ground, which made him resemble elements of nature, he fought, and came and went, with a sickle and a machete. One passage of the book ties the old man to the blood line, to the clan, to the "morality of the countryside": he knows everything, "a true man" (214).

The grandfather has a power given him by knowledge. He was the one who told his grandson the stories (such as those about crazy Rosa and Colonel Honorato) that now haunt him, lost in the city's corruption (214). Like Belmiro in Cyro dos Anjo's *O amanuense Belmiro,* Barra Mansa interrupts the clan's lineage and, like Belmiro and the poetic subject of Carlos Drummond de Andrade, he is a "fazendeiro of the air." In these characters, the patriarchal chain, as well as blood lines, are broken.

Observe these three passages: "that was the only point on which Orestes didn't agree with Pilates, or, to use their language, the string didn't fit the fiddle" (57); "without knowing it, *Mata-sete* was summarizing Aristotle" (95); "(since this story may well reach people unfamiliar with São Paulo slang, let it be explained that a 'parrot' is a piece of paper which in commercial accounting books is called a bill of exchange)" (151).

In the first, alluding to the friendship between Barra and his compadre, the narrator differentiates himself from the characters and their environment, showing himself to be educated and enlightened, which is confirmed in the second passage. In the third, he distinguishes himself from the reader, since he understands Paulista slang. We thus have an educated narrator who is familiar with São Paulo's small middle class, knows its language, and expresses concern about its problems. Differentiating the narrator from the other characters (and from the reader) perhaps risks the identification of the narrator with the author. To what extent, and I leave the question unanswered, is the novelist equally attracted to and imprisoned by the past?

I want to recall the nostalgic tone permeating the period's fiction and marking the biographies of several of the generation's writers, a number of whom were sons of great patriarchal families in decadence. In the fictional sphere, I evoke the sugarcane cycle of Lins do Rego or the indignation of the main character of *Angústia,* by Graciliano Ramos, with the shrinking of his name (Luís da Silva) when compared to that of his grandfather (Trajano Pereira de Aquino Cavalcante e Silva), an old senhor de engenho. The sympathy of these narrators for the dominated, which is responsible for the social orientation often attributed to their works, does not hide, as Luiz Costa Lima observes in another context, "their affective attraction to decaying manors," and their books are nourished by this contradiction ("Carlos Drummond de Andrade: memória e ficção," 173).

It is further necessary to emphasize that the book's title underlines the character of the grandfather, the old fazendeiro. Also, urban life is, in the final analysis, criticized as being traversed by the permanence of certain relationships (notably of married life) which are clear remnants of the patriarchal past. All of this leads me to include Galeão Coutinho's work in the nostalgic vein that misses the seignorial scene. "The good old days were those of Colonel José Paulino," we read in José Lins; "the good old days were those of Vovô Morungaba" is the regretful sigh that need not be murmured in this novel of 1938.

The succinct biographical note appended to the volume informs us that Galeão Coutinho frequented the library of the fazendeiro Otávio Denys, who "guided his first steps in the world of ideas" (Denys thus functions as the 'father,' passing knowledge to the 'son,' the future writer). In this he reproduces, with small variations, writers such as João Alphonsus, Graciliano Ramos, Lúcio Cardoso, and Cyro dos Anjos. In these writers' intellectual trajectories, the father (or his symbolic substitute), in whom the patriarchal masculine trunk is always weakened and who is often more of a dreamer and a man of letters than an effective "man of the land," attempts to reinforce his power through knowledge and pass along to his son a taste for reading and literature. In the beginning a form of evasion, the imaginary of the other's text is converted, in adulthood, into the imaginary articulated by the writer, who undertakes, in the space of literary representation, a search for the past, the paternal figure, the family clan, fictionally restoring the seignorial scene. More significant for my analysis, in the same note I read that Galeão Coutinho spent his childhood and the beginning of his adolescence in the Rio de Janeiro municipality of Pádua, and he once wrote that he suffered "nostalgia for the Fazenda Floresta," located "below the imposing Serra das Freixeiras," property of the fazendeiro Denys.

If the interpretation is correct, a small adjustment in Genolino Amado's assertion outlined earlier may be in order. The rural novel is not, in the final analysis, a libel against the social abandonment of the countryside, but rather a regretful song of the decadence of the "good old days." On the other hand, the urban novel of a Cyro dos Anjos or a Galeão Coutinho is not another literary vein, but rather the other side of the same coin: Brazilian literature of the 1930s is turned primarily toward the past, despite, as in the case of Coutinho, revealing the scars of the city in a phase of industrialization and modernization.

Before concluding, I would like to refer to a final detail about *Vovô Morungaba*. In her delirium, Barra's youngest daughter Cecília thinks she is pursued by an old man (and it is insinuated that it is Barra's grandfather), and we learn that she frequently goes to the movies and has the habit of reading Hollywood magazines (180). This is Cecília's favorite language, the cultural discourse of the urban space that is coming into being.

In opposition, there is a language of the singer in another story, this time of a fiddler, told by Vovô Morungaba to the young Barra Mansa: "He wrote verses that made stones cry" (176). And there is a language of birds, which, in his distant childhood, the protagonist had learned with his grandfather: "There was an intelligible language of birds" (215).[8] In contrast with the massive character of the daughter's preferred language, that of the past and the rural environment, the one linked to his grandfather, is poetic.

The decadence of that mythified world, deriving from the process of urbanization and transformation in the direction of modernity, implies an *absence of language:* I return to the micronarratives of crazy Rosa and Colonel Honorato. While the first was "mumbling nobody knew what" in the "exasperated soliloquies" of a language disturbance—madness—provoked by sudden poverty, the colonel, for identical reasons, simply becomes mute: "He just couldn't say anything. Some guttural sounds would come out of his throat, like a child when he begins to articulate simple words" (169).

If we consider that Abolition, the immediate cause of Rosa and Honorato's disgrace and the loss of language, accelerated the march of industrialization, urbanization, and modernization, we perceive that the emergence of the city corresponds to the decline of the countryside. When Cecília dies, two neighbors allude to her illness. One says that "a poor person's illness has no name. 'She caught something' . . . "; to which the other adds: "Whether rich or poor, when it is time to die, what good is a name?" (215). The final question of Galeão Coutinho's novel relates death to the loss of the name and of language.

III

I can now attempt to bring together the lines provided by the examination of these three narratives by Galeão Coutinho, as well as restate the conclusions advanced throughout the study.

Since his narrator is machista to the extreme, the masculine vision (which is prejudiced against women) that we find in the Brazilian novel prior to 1930 (and even after, as in Jorge Amado's *Gabriela, cravo e canela*) is restated. On the other hand, these texts tend to offer a critical angle on the present, but questioned carefully, they finally reveal a mythification of the seignorial past, returning nostalgically to the "good old days" in which the traditional values of the rural world predominated. In truth, the urban atmosphere in which they are set appears still bound to the agrarian and patriarchal heritage in a typical moment of *transition:* modernization has not been consolidated, just as the traditional order has not come completely undone. "When the urban environment appears, when the city begins to be formed, [. . .] already presenting the first manifestations of what we today call urban life, rural influences are projected onto them, giving them their initial contours" (Diégues, 121).

Galeão Coutinho seems to corroborate a constant detectable in other writers of the period, such as Graciliano, Lins do Rego, Lúcio Cardoso, Cyro dos Anjos, and João Alphonsus: they approach literature by way of a father (real or symbolic), who gives them knowledge, which is their power. The father gives them the talent of writing. Since these writers were frequently from decadent families, such knowledge permitted them, later, to recuperate the seignorial scene and the past in the space of fictional representation.

A literature of this kind tends to be emptied of its critical potential and becomes, rather, a restoration of a world that no longer exists. Or, said in another way: the affective compromise and the tone of sublimation such fiction ultimately adopts undermines its potential project of social criticism. This judgment, still current in the evaluation of these narrative texts, needs to be variegated. Being, in the final analysis, a recherche du temps perdu, one cannot see this fictional production as really problematizing the present. Instead, everything leads us to believe that it attempts to fill the absence provoked by the failure of the seignorial scene. With propriety Sérgio Miceli calls these writers "chroniclers of the murdered house," alluding to Lúcio Cardoso's novel, *Crônica da casa assassinada,* or "novelists of antique shops," an epithet borrowed from Mário de Andrade, who used it to discuss the works of Cornélio Penna (*Intelectuais e classe dirigente no Brasil,* 91, 93).

This reinserts Galeão Coutinho in Brazilian literary history, to the extent that his work is one more piece in the whole of 1930s fiction. That is: in it we see the same basic components detected in the so-called regionalists. Urban prose, far from constituting a difference in relation to the predominant rural vein, is rather another side of the same problem. It is a literature which looks at the present through a "rearview mirror" (Santiago, "Vale quanto pesa," 28), which ends up showing (again) the past. It is important, however, to consider it as an indispensable element for the understanding of the period's literary production in all its complexity: both the regional novel and the urban novel compose a fresco which, analyzed with care, reveals the conservative nature of Brazilian modernization.

Finally, the thesis I would like to reinforce can be formulated as follows: Brazilian literature (from 1850 until 1950), in its most general lines, is produced by a dominant landed elite, read basically by the same class, and deals, in the final analysis, with the same social segment (even when it apparently discusses the *other,* belonging to the periphery). From this results the impression that we are always reading the same story—that of the seignorial agrarian sectors and their decadence—as if the Brazilian novel of the *transition* only knew this same (self)portrait.

If the thesis is correct, we will not only have to rethink Brazilian literature of the 1930s, but also problematize the entire historicization of our literary patrimony, searching for those texts which tell the story of the *same* and those which, installing *difference,* escape from the dominant model. Restricting myself to the instant analyzed here, the various currents in which fictional production is divided seem to be no more than different sides of a single coin. The apparent lack of concern with which available compendia of Brazilian literature treat the diverse tendencies impedes the composition, at the end of their survey, of this mural that repeats the same, that insists on sending us back to the past of the seignorial manors, instead of making the reader face the modernization taking hold of Brazilian society in the 1930s.

In this sense, it would be important to put in parentheses even the assertion of Alfredo Bosi with which I opened this essay: to what extent does this narrative in fact draw a "historical and concrete," "contradictory" portrait of Brazil? Is the contradiction precisely in this "conservative modernization" that moves forward and looks backward? Since it is such a nostalgic literature, in what terms can one speak of its political contours? Does it manage to free itself from the process of mythification that Bosi sees in 1922? The study of Galeão Coutinho, as a representative of the urban prose of the 1930s, leaves us a series of questions. Furthermore: if one thinks of an intertextual dialogue between the literary phenomenon and social discourse, the question about the very trajectory of Brazilian society and its ruling elites remains up in the air, provoking reflections about its authoritarian and conservative nature.

I alluded to the coincidence between death and the loss of the name and of language at the end of the previous section. Paradoxically, to the inexorable decline of the patriarchal landowners and rulers the literature of the *period of transition* responded with so many stories that tell us this very same plot. However, on the horizon of these texts there beats a silence, provoked by the breaking of the "pearl necklace" referred to in the epigraph of this study. This sentence from Galeão Coutinho's 1938 novel assumes a contour of truth: "Behind all of that was the old Morungaba" (182). That is: behind all this literature is the seignorial past, weighing on the shoulders of the modernization of Brazilian society. Starting from this assertion one can reread a great deal of Brazil's literary production, in which urban or regionalist writers, telling ultimately the same story, attempt to gather the pearls of a broken necklace in the imaginary space of fiction.

All History Is Remorse —Toward a Reading of Modernist Poetry

> Like a fly, the poetic word is attracted by the sugar that it had earlier refused, but which never ceases to attract it.
>
> —*Luiz Costa Lima*

I

In a recent study of Mário de Andrade's poetry, João Luiz Lafetá analyzes the problematics of *A costela do Grão Cão* and *O livro azul,* establishing a link between the search for an individual identity and the search for a group identity: "Mário's poetry is a set of reflections (transposed to the artistic level) about the various problems that comprised the ideological universe of the Brazilian bourgeoisie's lettered elite during these twenty-five years [1920–1945]. The poet's various masks correspond to precise instants of the bourgeoisie's ideological movements and constitute true crystallizations of the self-image that it had attempted to create" (*Figuração da intimidade,* 15).

Lafetá shows that this social group had lost its euphoria and confidence and that the crises that divided the lettered elite's consciousness began after the Revolution of 1930, when the structures of the Old Republic were dismantled and a vacuum opened for the bourgeoisie. The road had already been chosen—the development of capital—but it did not appear clearly in the minds of the participants of the process. At this moment of *transition* in Brazilian society, there begins a crisis of hegemony, reflected in difficult disputes concerning the definition of the State (197–98).

Lafetá suggests that there then occurred a rejection of History in Mário's poetry, and he detects a "curious attitude of negation, from a modern poet who attempted to exorcise the bases of capitalist modernity: movement, life in chronological time, the transformative activity of the world. The alternative proposed is rest, alienation from time, inactivity, everything that signifies a retreat of the libido from objects and its reabsorption in the indifferent world of the id" (210).

In this sense, Mário's poetry ultimately assumes a very primitive religious meaning (210), pointing toward a ritual repetition of myth, suspending chronological and linear time, inscribing itself in the internal circularity of return, and opposing the profane universe of History, substituting the ruinous situation before him with limitless contemplation (211). According to Lafetá, in subsequent manifestations of Mário's poetry (which he does not deal with in this essay), the poet develops the theme of class struggle, focusing on the country's reality.

Lafetá's extremely suggestive study provokes the following reflection: would it not be possible to track the same *absence of History*—understood as a discursive inscription—in other modernist poets (and prose writers)? If we examined the poetic production of the 1920s and 1930s as a whole, searching for similarities, would we not find the same perplexity in a group of intellectuals, related biographically or ideologically to the decadent agrarian aristocracy or to the incipient bourgeoisie, who were beginning to understand that the direction taken by the country and by the increasingly capitalist State was, in a certain sense, marginalizing them, leaving them defenseless in the process of modernization which, in one way or another, their literary production had attempted to incorporate and stimulate?

The question is fascinating, and in this text I propose merely to outline it. From the outset we might think, in very precarious terms, of the eternity that pervades Murilo Mendes,[1] the escape to Pasárgada and the frustration of a "whole life that could have been but was not" that stigmatizes Bandeira,[2] Vinicius de Moraes's search for the Great Mother,[3] Cecília Meireles's mysticism,[4] the religious turn or the repeated racial prejudice in Jorge de Lima,[5] or Cassiano Ricardo's "projection of the ideological."[6] It is not a question of imposing a straitjacket on such poets nor of suggesting that the jettisoning of History from their texts invalidates their poetry.

Such a strategy, rather, would result in a more complete understanding of these poets and their production in terms of their interaction with the moment in which they lived. This kind of approach would contribute greatly to a better understanding of Brazilian Modernism, of modernists as intellectuals, and of the process of Brazilian society's modernization, with all of its contradictions. It would also be important, among other things, to examine the involvement of some of them, such as Vinicius, Ricardo, or Drummond, with the Estado Novo, either through DIP or the Capanema ministry.[7]

Once the backbone of this critical examination is established, I believe that figures such as Oswald de Andrade, with his parodic poems that reread Brazil's past or with his participatory lyricism,[8] or João Cabral de Melo Neto, with his constructive and sharpened anti-lyrics, whose teeth cut through the "severinidade sem plumas" of the northeastern social fabric,[9] would gain a surprising salience, as if provoking a rearrangement in the canonical vision of modernist poetry. If my reasoning is correct, both would be inscribed in the path of History, at a moment when disdain for historicity seemed to shape poetic production. Because in these works History becomes a problem and there is a circulation of meaning (Oswald's short poems about Brazilian history are, once again, a good example).

As a means of outlining this kind of reading, I will briefly examine the work of Carlos Drummond de Andrade, presupposing that his poetry, taken as a whole, composes a vast mural narrating the trajectory of the same poetic subject, created through language.[10] Drummond serves my purposes well since, as José Guilherme Merquior once wrote, his personal adventure—"*the son of a fazendeiro who became a bureaucrat in a big city*"—coincides with Brazil's social evolution (*Verso universo em Drummond,* 48). Antonio Candido has noted his surprise with Drummond's poetry by affirming that "it is no doubt curious that the greatest social poet of our contemporary literature is, at the same time, the great singer of tradition and of the family as a group" (*Vários escritos,* 110).

Criticism of Carlos Drummond de Andrade either analyzes some of his texts in isolation (losing, as a result, a complete vision of the journey undertaken by the lyrical self), or focuses on the whole of his work but from an eminently stylistic perspective (Hélcio Martins's study of his rhyme and Gilberto Mendonça Teles's examination of the stylistics of repetition might be the best examples) or from a thematic-formal one (Affonso Romano de Sant'Anna's study of the "gauche" in time; the chapter about the "corrosion-principle" in Luiz Costa Lima's *Lira e antilira;* John Gledson's book-length study). A sociohistorical approach to Drummond which would insert him in the more general panorama of a sociology of modernist intellectuals thus seems to be lacking.

II

John Gledson suggests that Drummond's poetry can be seen as an extensive questioning about the world's meaning. His analysis focuses on "the relations between the poet and the multiple objective structures—social, linguistic, family, literary, existential, economic, historical, etc.—by which he knew himself limited, but which he is, naturally, incapable of describing and much less dominating. In their varied structures, his poems represent diverse stages in an attempt to capture and understand them" (17).

As we know, the Brazilian *transition* brings with it a rearrangement of the ruling classes and eventually dislodges the almost isolated agrarian oligarchies linked to exports and forces them to share power with other fractions of the dominant classes, notably the urban-industrial bourgeoisie. While they enjoyed hegemony, large landowners perpetrated an authoritarian discourse that shaped the production of meaning about the country's reality which was always decodified in relation to their interests. The changes brought by the Republic were summarized by a simple "change of signboards," as one of Machado de Assis's characters ironically remarks, since the new political system was organized according to the old seignorial segment's desire for continuity, without resulting in a more substantial transformation. The alternation in power synthesized in the política dos governadores and the "coffee-and-milk" formula translates into an accommodation of the republican institutional order with the purposes of the planters. Later, in 1930, these classes would receive a greater blow, brought about by dissident oligarchies, such as those in Rio Grande do Sul and São Paulo, who were dissatisfied with the nomination of Júlio

Prestes and allied with foreign capital and the bourgeoisie, with their project to modernize the country through industrialization.

The task of consolidating a "nationalist," centralizing, and authoritarian Brazilian State was consummated in 1937 with the Estado Novo dictatorship, in which military sectors such as the tenentes participated. Still, the sedimentation of the national State could not be successful without a tacit agreement between the emergent groups and those who intimately knew the secrets of power and domination, such as planters. This alliance is to a great extent responsible for the most acute contradictions of Brazilian modernization, which becomes compromised with the past and with the traditional order that it had proposed to revoke. As Sérgio Buarque de Holanda has noted, "The Brazilian State preserves some of the external forms of the traditional system as respectful relics, after the base that supported it disappeared: a periphery without a center" (131). The center, in this case, would be the hegemonic agrarian system, now in the process of being replaced by the State.

The discourse generated by hegemonic oligarchies overdetermined Brazilian culture and society prior to 1930, and, experiencing the commotion occasioned by the collapse of hegemony, with the Revolution of 1930, elements from this social group became disoriented when they perceived that the values of their class no longer found total historical support and that the world promised by the emergent capitalist order did not yet fully exist in the context of the *transition*. Thus a crisis begins for these subjects who are no longer central protagonists of the social dynamic and who need to find a different form of participation in the new political panorama. Such crises affect primarily the lettered elite, as Lafetá has suggested.

Discussing the formation of the urban middle fractions, Décio Saes contributes to a better understanding of the phenomenon: the old, bankrupt, small landowners, he affirms, are pushed toward the cities, "where they begin to occupy the more elevated positions in the bureaucratic apparatus and to fulfill the most qualified services," taking charge, for example, of the liberal professions. These sectors are traversed by "the cult of traditional values, a stratified vision of social reality, and a superestimation of their social status [. . .]. Even impoverished, the members of these groups see themselves as aristocrats, which establishes an effective and valorative link to still economically powerful traditional groups" (*Classe média e política na Primeira República,* 34). From this results their identification, by way of social and family ties and economic dependency, with the rural aristocracy (34).

We now have another face of the problem, which shows how much the growing urban middle classes, derived from ruined sectors of the patriarchal agrarian system, join the still powerful oligarchical aristocracy, imposing continuity rather than rupture. Co-opted by sentimental sympathy and/or financial subjection, they do not assume a dissonant posture. Neither do they free themselves from their commitment to the past, remaining literally without a relevant social role to play as secondary actors in the pact of 1930 (we know that, later on, many intellectuals will participate in the Estado Novo apparatus).

Drummond's poetry undertakes a reading of this crisis. It stages the drama of a poetic subject coming from a rural universe who moves to the urban environment and is transformed into a "fazendeiro of the air" (the metaphor that entitles one of his collections of poems). The crisis of Drummond's poetic subject transcends the individual plane and coincides with the crisis of a social subject (the failed oligarchies) and of intellectuals in the 1930s. The being shaped in language inquires about the meaning of the "world's machine," painfully experiences urban space and modernity, asks about man's raison d'être, solitary and without love in the large city and the contemporary scenario (in the poem "Elegia 1938" ["Elegy 1938"], for example, the world is old, and the text emphasizes the possibility of dynamiting Manhattan island [59–60]).

This subject is unable to face the ultimate meaning of the reality that surrounds him not only because it does not declare itself to him but also because he has lost the code, the system of references, that would allow him to interpret the world. The center is empty, the father (as the origin of meaning) is dead. The code he has lost is that of his class, discarded from its leading position in the Brazilian historical flow, which creates an atmosphere of tension in Drummond's poetry.

In this sense, the Drummondian "gauche" is not merely displaced, as modern man might be understood. The anjo torto (crooked angel) who appears in "Poema de sete faces" (["Poem with Seven Faces"] in *Reunião,* 3),[11] which inaugurates his work, does not merely confer on Carlos the "marginality of the man and the poetry," inverting the text of the annunciation and restating another biblical passage, that of the fallen angels, expelled from paradise (Walty and Campos, 73). He is also the individual thrown from his class (obliged to share power), deprived of a code to clarify the world, perplexed in the face of a reality that makes no sense and for which he does not have a system of signification capable of explaining it.

It is no coincidence that the next poem which attributes the status of gauche to the Drummondian poetic subject is "Infância" (["Childhood"], 3–4), a text that shows the lyrical self excluded from the family space, secluded between two mango trees and immersed in reading the adventures of Robinson Crusoe. If the "Poema de sete faces" raised the question of identity, in "Infância" the lyrical self is identified with someone else's imaginary, through language, or with a black maid who calls him for coffee. In both cases, he does not recognize himself in the family environment, but rather in those who are unlike him. In the family, as later in the big city, the gauche is alone. And his story, which can be followed throughout Drummond's poetry, is given as (another) fiction in the green and black space (of the mango trees and the maid's voice, respectively), a true island of pleasure.[12]

From this moment on, childhood and its corollaries—the past, the family, the paternal figure, and the native town—undergo a process of repression in the Drummondian text, appearing sporadically but with increasing frequency, until assuming a preponderant presence in the explicit memorialism of *Boitempo* and *Menino antigo*. At first, references to the family ("Família" ["Family"], 20) are caustic. The rural town ("Cidadezinha qualquer" ["Any Little Town"], 17) and the traditional family are characterized as spaces of repetition and lack of dynamism: "só um mosquito rápido / mostra inquietação" (["only a darting mosquito / shows any restlessness"] "Sesta" ["Siesta"], 25). Itabira, the poet's hometown, a complex signifier in Drummond's poetry, is also initially painted as somnolent, in the fourth section of "Lanterna mágica" (["Magic Lantern"], 9).

The Drummondian poetic subject already finds itself in the big city in "Poema de sete faces." In this environment, his search for the other will encounter disaffection, with the dance of love (as in

"Quadrilha" ["Quadrille"] and "Não se mate" ["Don't Kill Yourself"], 19 and 40) which cannot compensate for the emptiness of the amorous being destined to love (see poems such as "A bruxa" ["The Witch"], "O elefante" ["The Elephant"], and "Amar" ["To Love"], 63, 105–6, and 174, respectively). Bourgeois institutions are the object of irony in poems such as "Sociedade" (["Society"], 23–24). Gradually, the lack of surprise and madness takes over the city, as in "Privilégio do mar" (["Privilege of the Sea"], 50). City and country are even compared in "O boi" (["The Ox"], 63–64), both presenting an identical sameness.

Interwoven with the texts that tell of solitude in the city are others that thematize the past. "Confidência do itabirano" (["Itabiran Confession"], 45) places the reader before a painful portrait on the wall. "Tristeza do Império" (["The Empire's Sadness"], 47) reveals a seignorial substratum, also evident in "Iniciação amorosa" (["Amorous Initiation"], 22), which relates his sexual initiation with a black washerwoman, as well as in the poem "Infância." "Os mortos de sobrecasaca" (["The Dead in Frock Coats"], 49–50) describes a photograph worn by time, which emits a paradoxical sigh of life—but the dead are still unnamed.

Drummond's poetic text outlines the generating nucleus of his poetry. Time is a corrosive, destructive element with its inexorable passing ("Dentaduras duplas" ["Double Dentures"], 56).[13] Despite its action, however, a residue element always remains, a "falta que ama" ("a lack that loves") which ends up being the motivating element of Drummond's poetry. In "Passagem do ano" (["Year's End"], 87–88), "o corpo gasto renova-se em espuma" ("the tired body renews itself with lather"); in "Resíduo" ("Residue"), "de tudo fica um pouco" (["of everything a little remained"], 102–3); in "Permanência" (["Permanence"], 191), "o que [. . .] fomos um dia / [. . .] contudo arde em nós" ("what [. . .] we once were / [. . .] still burns within us"); in "Os poderes infernais" (["Infernal Powers"], 221), "o meu amor é tudo que, morrendo, / não morre todo, e fica no ar, parado" ("My love is everything that, when it dies / it does not die completely, remaining still in the air"); in "O enterrado vivo" (["Buried Alive"], 206), "sempre no meu sempre a mesma ausência" ("always in my always the same absence").

The poems gradually begin to thematize the clan, the father,

Itabira, the past, terms that mix and are inscribed under the same sign of corrosion ("Viagem na família," "No país dos Andrades," "A mesa" ["Travelling in the Family," "In the Country of the Andrades," "The Table"], 72–74, 125, and 194–97),[14] and the poet reveals his nostalgia, as in "Lembrança do mundo antigo" (["Souvenir of the Ancient World"], 59)—"não havia perigo" ("there was no danger")—or in the peaceful apotheosis that closes "Os rostos imóveis" (["Motionless Faces"], 68–70). In "Retrato de família" (["Family Portrait"], 117), the photograph is a residue that seems to resist the action of time, in a movement in which some things wither but others are proposed, and the dead are transformed, revived by poetic language.

In "Encontro" (["Encounter"], 193), the poetic subject writes, "meu pai perdi no tempo e ganho em sonho" ("I lost my father in time, but find him in dreams"), giving the father an air of eternity (his gray fields are moistened by a river that runs beyond time); in "Memória" (["Memory"], 168), a verse stresses that things that are finished remain, and he loves that which is lost; in "Perguntas" (["Questions"], 192), he leans worriedly over the "restos de restos" ("remains of remains") in order to *"amar, depois de perder"* (*"love, after losing"*). As we read in "Remissão" (["Remission"], 164), memory is the food of Drummond's poetry.

In fact, even in the texts which are not explicitly memorialistic, the generating process of Drummond's poetry has a memorialistic contour, since it germinates in the residual lack that remains after the implacable corrosion of time. Nothing is left, except words: little by little, the Drummondian text undertakes a recovery, through poetic discourse, of the past, the family, the patriarchal clan, and the father. The dead live only in us ("Convívio" ["Familiarity"], 190) and in language. The paradox of a poetry that is written starting from a lack is manifested even in the oxymoronic structure of many verses: "tudo vivido? Nada. / Nada vivido? Tudo" ("everything lived? Nothing. / Nothing lived? Everything"); the "poesia mais rica / é um sinal de menos" (["richest poetry / is a minus sign"] "Poema-orelha" ["Flap-Poem"], 219).

The poet who sang the present in "Os ombros suportam o mundo" (["Shoulders Bear the World"], 55), without having found an identification with the other in love or in the worker ("O operário no mar" ["The Worker at Sea"], 47–48), returns in a "volta [d]o filho pródigo / à casa do pai / e o próprio pai é morto desde Adão" (["the return of the prodigal son / to his father's house / and the father himself has been dead since Adam"] "Remate" ["Conclusion"], 258). And his text begins to celebrate the eternal ("Eterno" ["Eternal"], 209–10) or to establish new ancestors ("Como um presente" ["Like a Present"], 117–19).

At this moment, poetically reencountering the father, things seem to acquire a meaning they did not have before: in the poem "Comunhão" (["Communion"] *Boitempo,* 161), the poetic subject occupies the empty space among the dead and everything is illuminated. Identification is created with the remaining components of the clan. With the restoration of the father, the family, and the past, which are treated with a certain affection and irony in works after *Boitempo* (1968),[15] the code is recovered—the norms of the traditional family—through the repetition of ancestral models, bound to the bloodline and the patriarchal universe. It did no good to flee from the scorpion, because it governs and dictates meanings which are predetermined from the beginning ("Signo" ["Sign"], *Boitempo,* 77). Knowledge itself and the language used to undertake this journey of poetic return to Itabira are paternal gifts: "Escritório" (["Office"] *Menino antigo,* 80) speaks of the dictionary, and "Biblioteca verde" (["Green Library"] *Menino antigo,* 124) recalls the father's present, an encylopedia, whose color refers us to the privileged space among the mango trees of "Infância," showing that, through this intimate seam, he was not an island so distant from his father or, and this is another hypothesis, that having taken refuge there was ultimately a way to return.

The repetition of the father in Drummond does not occur as a *difference.* We have seen that the father has been dead since Adam. In the poem "Janela" (["Window"], 269) the faded red leaves of the almond tree are the same, original, archetypical leaves of before. The text does not recognize that each leaf is the same and another at the same time. The cyclical character of nature is sustained in the tension between the same and the other. Those critics who have praised the social poet of *A rosa do povo* spoke too soon, since the complete works of Drummond free themselves from the present and turn toward the eternal, toward the father, and toward a code that elides difference and cultivates the identical.

III

In a study of the Brazilian family, Jurandir Freire Costa shows that the family was the epicenter of the father's power. Discussing the nature of family relations, he writes:

> In the Colony, to survive, expand, or progress were synonymous with repetition. The wise and efficient father was the one who managed to reproduce, with the greatest possible fidelity, his ancestors' formula of domination. The material solidity of property depended on this knowledge deriving from the oral tradition and his own experience. The old was more important than the new. The country's cultural backwardness did not permit the circulation of technical innovations. Useful information came from the past. Family life was a permanent exercise in listening to what had gone by, and the head of the household was the translator and spokesman of his ancestors' lessons. (*Ordem médica e norma familiar,* 158)

If the preceding considerations are valid, the repetitive tendency noted in Drummond leads us to a traditional way of life, to an archaic form of wisdom, questioned in the period of *transition* referred to previously. In this sense, History is absent, neutralized, frozen in eternity, transformed into *remorse* ("Museu da Inconfidência" ["Museum of the Inconfidência"], 183), regretting the past, which time corroded into a residual and memory, and repentant for loving that which was lost. The present, euphorically celebrated in the middle of his work, is diluted in a cyclical return. History, seen as a possibility of transformation, is empty. The Drummondian text ends up not finding the *other* (poems about amorous interaction are rare),[16] sheltering itself in a redundant identical. The nonalterity becomes ahistorical. The father he seeks is a copy, a simulacrum; he is the Law, to be imitated and followed, an Ur-code that illuminates the world and the circle in which the subject reoccupies his place. In Drummond, the individual level of the search for the father and the social level of the restoration of the patriarchal Brazilian past coincide. This is also the drama of the period's intelligentsia.

If this analysis, concentrating on Drummond as a paradigm of modernist poetry, is correct, then I would disagree with Renato

Ortiz when he writes: "Modernism is considered by many to be a point of reference because this cultural movement brought with it an historical awareness that until then was found only diffusely in society" (40). Everything leads us to believe that this is a mere epidermic facet of the problem or, in the best of hypotheses, that it does not apply indiscriminately to Modernism as a whole.

All this seems problematic if we keep in mind that the process of modernization that Brazilian society was undergoing, and to which Carlos Drummond de Andrade's poetry was so often attentive, demanded a historical vision necessarily implying change. What remains, as a residual of reading, despite the high quality attained by poems such as "Passagem do ano" (["Year's End"], 87–88) or "Campo de flores" (["Field of Flowers"], 178), is the same sensation of suffocating immobility that afflicts a significant part of modernist intellectual production. The Drummondian text lives the crisis of its time in a dramatic fashion, but the solution that it seems to present, in terms of its exile in language, is that of the immutable. The bad odor of memory that is emitted and which the poet tries unsuccessfully to suppress ("Resíduo" ["Residue"], 103) does not destroy that which is consummated: "muito mais que lindas, / essas ficarão" (["much more than beautiful things / they will remain"] "Memória," 168). Thus, all History can only be remorse.

The Map of the Map-of-the-Map —Modernity in Érico Veríssimo

> In the usual improvisation of literary studies in Brazil, the same thing normally occurs with *O tempo e o vento* that happens with James Joyce's *Ulysses* and João Guimarães Rosa's *Grande sertão: veredas:* almost everyone cites them, but few have read them.
>
> —*Flávio Loureiro Chaves*

I

O tempo e o vento is one of the most important works of Brazilian literature.[1] Even the sensation of some prolixity does not affect the impact of this mural woven through the 2,295 pages that narrate the saga of the Terra Cambará family, written and published during fourteen years. Érico Veríssimo shares with Jorge Amado the fortune of being a widely translated writer with broad popular acceptance, but one who, in contrast, does not receive a critical acclaim on the level of his public popularity and the strength of his literature. Such disdain in no way corresponds to his work's relevance. The fact that essayists from Veríssimo's home state of Rio Grande do Sul are the ones who have dedicated most attention to him should not lead us to the false conclusion of "provincialism." And, even taking these studies into account, there is still the need of understanding the fiction of the author of *Incidente em Antares*.[2]

I do not intend to scrutinize the entire vast mural Veríssimo elaborates in *O tempo e o vento*. Rather, I will emphasize his modernity, especially in comparison with his contemporaries, since he professes a more open vision in the nostalgic and reactionary context that stigmatizes a good part of the generation of 1930s narrative production.

II

Situating Veríssimo's fiction in the literature of the 1930s, Flávio Loureiro Chaves has written the following:

> Much of the novel of the 1930s was regionalist because its entrance into the debate about the social crisis made it a direct participant, either by attempting to document it through a naturalist prism (as occurred with José Américo de Almeida), or by intentionally assuming a partisan connotation. We understand by partisan here not only openly pamphletary literature (such as much of the first phase of Jorge Amado), but also that which, under the pretext of writing an elegy of the past or recording folklore and local customs, ended up defining an ultra-reactionary position which, in its conservatism, could not disguise an attempt to recuperate a time that was historically dead. (*Érico Veríssimo: realismo e sociedade,* 33–34)

For Chaves, Veríssimo did not stop with regionalism, precisely because he was interested in investigating human beings and their fate and distinguishing, in the episodic, the reflection of the human condition. Veríssimo's observation of the regional implied the revelation of the social, and he journeyed from a critique of a regional society to a problematization of History and a discussion of the drama of contemporary society (34, 134). Chaves further notes the non-nostalgic character of Veríssimo's historical reflections on the patriarchal past.

Despite his differences, Veríssimo's work shares a number of constants detectable in the literature of the 1930s. The presence of a seignorial, masculine, and patriarchal order is clear. Consequently, women are oppressed figures, Penelopes waiting for their men to return from battle. The men, involved in border wars or in internal struggles, are all-powerful, entitled to become involved with lovers or prostitutes.[3] On the other hand, white women of a certain social standing are wives, the object of a spiritualized love while mestizas and the socially less favored are used for male sexual satisfaction. In this hierarchical society power derives from the possession of land.

Still in consonance with other texts of the period, the world of the old rural, Gaúcho patriarchy suffers a decline throughout the trilogy. Suffice it to note the titles: *O continente* corresponds to the mythical foundation of Rio Grande do Sul, with an authentic, epic southern wind blowing in its pages; *O retrato* shows us the disequilibrium introduced by Rodrigo Cambará, who goes to study in Porto Alegre, the capital city, an "urban animal" who returns to Santa Fé armed with ideas of change with the purpose of civilizing the province and in whom the Sobrado clan is fractured; *O arquipélago*, which presents us a Rodrigo between life and death, signals the shattering of the rural aristocracy's traditional values, which are already degraded in the main character, and brings into the discussion the various "islands" in which the continent had been fragmented, along with the resulting dilemmas. In this regard, Rodrigo has a difficult relationship with his father (which is replicated in Floriano, his son), and he thus also re-casts protagonists of various of the period's novels and memoirs.

Through this brief summary, we see points of contact between *O tempo e o vento* and the memorialistic or fictional work of José Lins do Rego, Graciliano Ramos, Cyro dos Anjos, Lúcio Cardoso, Cornélio Penna, João Alphonsus, Humberto de Campos, Galeão Coutinho, Autran Dourado, Adonias Filho, and Guimarães Rosa, among others, all of whom are either predecessors, participants, or heirs of the literary universe created in the 1930s. The affinities extend even to aspects of their biographical trajectories: the testimony "O escritor diante do espelho" ("The writer in front of the mirror") and the memoirs reveal that the Veríssimo who most affected the writer was his father, like him a dreamer, with whom he maintained a problematic relationship and in whose office he found magazines that made it possible for him to escape to a fantasy world. One further perceives a memorialistic substratum, as tenuous as it may be: the fact that in his family, women are more energetic than men provides him with the model for characters such as Ana Terra, Bibiana, and Maria Valéria, as well as for the correlated weakness of Bolivar or Rodrigo. Episodes such as that of Lieutenant Mello are similar to that of Bernardo Quaresma, in the novel. In many ways Rodrigo Cambará resembles Veríssimo's father, and the father-son relationship in real life is repeated in Floriano's conflict with Rodrigo: not only is the love scene with Cordélia reduplicated in *O tempo e o vento*, but also Floriano's dialogue with Rodrigo, at the end of *O arquipélago*, is a sublimating symbolic solution, a "settling of accounts" that, as Veríssimo writes, "I would like to have had with my own father" ("O escritor," 130).[4]

In all of this, I see similarities between *O tempo e o vento* and the literary production of the 1930s: the dominance of patriarchal values; the treatment of women and the separation between spiritual love and physical love, between white women and mestizas, and related to social status; an extremely hierarchical society; a portrait of the rural aristocracy's decadence; the dissonance brought by a character who had been educated in the city; problematic father-son relationships, both on the level of characters and in the writer's biography; a memorialistic substratum.

III

O tempo e o vento, however, also reveals incompatibilities with the established patterns of the fiction that was its contemporary, starting with the non-nostalgic nature referred to earlier. The fact that the paradigmatic texts are permeated by nostalgia—and I am thinking especially of José Lins do Rego's sugarcane cycle—contaminates them with a mythical atmosphere. The mythic appears to fill an absence in the dimensions of historical reality. It is in this sense that there exists a mythical ground in a book more directly planted in 1920s Modernism, such as *Macunaíma*—the adventures of the "hero without a character" points toward an eternal present, toward an originary primitivism, a preindustrial and precapitalist Brazil. In analogous fashion, the gradual disappearance of the hegemonic patriarchal classes will make writers restore them in the space of literary representation, mythically recuperating the seignorial scene. Along these lines, I refer the reader to novels such as Galeão Coutinho's *Vovô Morungaba* or Autran Dourado's *Ópera dos mortos*.[5]

From the epigraph and the title,[6] *O tempo e o vento* is based on the contradictory tension between permanence and change, between myth and history,[7] tradition and transitoriness. This polarity is reproduced diegetically to the extent that the female character, as Chaves has pointed out, symbolizes "the force of preservation," the "support of a world that threatens to collapse" (*O contador de histórias,* 77). In the final analysis, still according to Chaves, the trilogy relates the myth of life being reborn from the ashes, the warriors' self-destruction, and the women as a force for the conservation of the bloodline (80).[8]

The final implication of this tense bipolarity inverts the dominant fictional model of the 1930s, since *O tempo e o vento* ends up being, to rely again on Chaves, the "passage from mythical space to historical duration": "It is a question of accompanying man's trajectory *after* the rupture of the mythical universe, questioning, therefore, the meaning of his actions and his destiny in the historical, that is, social, world" (*Realismo e sociedade,* 84).

The process seems crucial for progressing in our reading of the trilogy. This tense structure is interwoven with another that I would call contrapuntal. It is worth recalling that Veríssimo translated Huxley's *Point Counter-Point,* published in 1933, the same year as *Clarissa.* Going against the predominant tendency of the period's intelligentsia to venerate French culture, Veríssimo, like Machado de Assis before him, became familiar with English-language literature and assimilated its fragmentary construction, which he uses beginning with *Caminhos cruzados.*

He perfects the technique in *O continente,* in which temporal planes and narrative foci alternate, thus releasing a diversity of voices and versions in the novel which do not cease even in the few moments when the focus is heterodiegetic, in the third person. The technique finds its most polished formulation, significantly, in the volume relating the dissolution of the Terra Cambará clan, especially in the six parts ironically titled "Family Reunion." In them the novel discusses and counterposes—without allowing one hierarchically to dominate the others—the various options and paths that arise from the bankruptcy of their world, from the values incarnate in Rodrigo, and the crisis the country experienced after 1930 during the Vargas period. There is the version of Rodrigo himself, sick in bed awaiting his final hour; the version of doctor Terêncio, representing reactionary ranchers who attempted to preserve Gaúcho traditions in a rather retrograde fashion; the communist version of Eduardo; Brother Toríbio's Catholic version; and the anarchistic and skeptical version of Roque Bandeira, which coexists with that of Jango, still bound to Angico and rural life; that of Maria Valéria, the heir of her ancestor, the valiant Ana Terra, reigning over Sobrado from the throne of her rocking chair; that of Sílvia, the woman who finds God; that of the futile couple Bibi and Sandoval; that of the deceased Bio, the last of the authentic Cambarás; that of the secular Liroca, a survivor of the siege of the mansion. As a point of unstable equilibrium, Floriano personifies a "third position," which can be synthesized in the formula with which he characterizes his project: "The solution for the 'islands' is for them to unite with each other, but without losing their dignity and identity as individuals" (Veríssimo, *O arquipélago,* 1:223). In other words, the trilogy, from the "continent" to the "archipelago," abandons monologism and embraces dialogism, in a trajectory from myth to History.

This trajectory, in turn, is articulated in a dialectical process that alternates reduction with amplification. If on the one hand the three volumes move from an inquest on regional society to a problematization of History and an understanding of the contemporary drama (Chaves, *Realismo e sociedade,* 134), extrapolating from the regional to the national and the universal, on the other hand the centuries of history covered by the trilogy are miniaturized in the particular saga of the Terra Cambarás. The historicity that traverses *O tempo e o vento* is thus animated by a movement of retraction/expansion, permitting the scrutiny of the great background mural (from the mid-eighteenth century until the end of the 1940s) at the same time it is condensed in the history of a single family. Consequently, the novel is and is not historical, and it undertakes the trajectory from the compact world of myth to the antagonisms and crossroads of History, an archipelago in which the bifurcations occasioned by the family's decline and the very impasse of modern, urban, and industrial Brazil, recently freed from the Estado Novo, coexist with those of the contemporary world, divided then by a crisis of values and threatened by the cold war, by totalitarianism, and by the atomic bomb.

History, in *O tempo e o vento,* thus suffers a reduction in terms of the narrated events, subjected to a criterion of selection, besides having been summarized in the family saga. But, simultaneously, it is dilated, just as the history of the Terra Cambarás and of Santa Fé is, on a smaller scale, the history of Brazil, especially of the Vargas period, and the symbol of the difficulties of contemporary man, divided by the loss of individual freedom.

The trilogy's backbone, again, is rendered concrete on the level of the characters: Captain Rodrigo is degraded in his grandson Rodrigo Cambará, while Ana Terra remains in Bibiana and continues in Maria Valéria. Time and the wind.

IV

The dynamic play described in the previous section finds its maximum consummation in the narrative's cyclical nature: on the last page, the reader perceives that the novelist Floriano follows the advice of Tio Bicho—"search for the bluebird in our own backyard"—and plans to write about his family and Rio Grande do Sul. The book we have just finished reading is the one Floriano begins to compose; the last paragraph of *O arquipélago* is identical to the initial paragraph of *O continente.* We are sent back to the beginning of the trilogy whenever we reach its end. The mirror is total: from myth to History, from the beginning to the end, from the regional to the universal, amplification-reduction, time and the wind, change and permanence, from the plot to the novel—and vice versa.

When we question Brazilian cultural discourse, the tendency toward monolithic versions leaps before our eyes, that is, the preponderance of one signification, the monovalence of meaning—as we know, literary production has mainly circulated among the elites, and popular manifestations were marginalized. An analysis of this cultural discourse shows how the version of the colonizer supplants that of the colonized; how that of the landed elites prevails over that of other social segments; how that of the State is imposed on local power; how centralization suffocates pluralization. Or, said another way, the archaeology of the Brazilian cultural discourse, at least the one generated by upper social segments, seems to evidence a constant conflict between the authoritarianism of the central power—represented by the Portuguese Crown during the colonial period, by large landowners during the Empire, by the State beginning with the Second Republic—and the voices of *difference.*

Therefore, the study of our social formation, momentarily discarding its nuances and historical complexity and seen in its underlying structure, truly seems to rest on the variable outlined. The very shape of Brazilian society, especially prior to the *transition,* before the turn of the century, implies the concept of centrality, since it can be configured in terms of *concentric circles.* In the center is the landowner from whom power emanates, who also plays the dual roles of father and man. From there to the periphery, always based on relations of hierarchy and domination, grounded on the one hand in the master-slave relationship and on the other in the patriarchal family, other relations are established in such a way that the individual's position is always given in reference to the center. During the existence of coronelismo it was common for farmhands and tenant farmers to define their place in the social structure as "Colonel Doe's people."

Leaving the Brazilian context for a moment, I would suggest that the pluralism of voices is characteristic of modernity, as are the decentering of truth, dialogism, the vertiginous play of meaning, always displaced and without beginning or end. *Don Quijote* is a modern novel primarily because it comports diverse versions of its episodes. Machado de Assis is extremely modern because he undermines hierarchies, relativizing values, in the same way that Borges's dream always refers back to another dream.

Starting with the fragmentation of *O arquipélago, O tempo e o vento* includes reflections about language and the dispersion of meaning, parallel to the multifaceted structure analyzed in previous sections. If the affirmation that reality is not verbal (*O arquipélago,* 2:381) does not take into account the fact that the real is discursive, later, in the metapoetic considerations of the "Caderno de pauta simples," Floriano writes that "in terms of language, the abyss has no bottom and we never stop falling" (400). Tio Bicho says that Rodrigo is "this and a million other things. What he was yesterday he no longer is today" (393).

In the final volume of *O arquipélago* we read passages such as these: "our adaptation to the real world occurs through words" (3:861); "if we compare the testimony of ten people about Rodrigo Cambará, we will see that there are great and small discrepancies between them, since each one will have felt and interpreted the man in his own way" (3:999). The synthesis of these reflections is interwoven with the architecture of the novel itself in this passage from the "Caderno":

> Semanticists affirm that the ideal map would be that which contained a map of itself, which in turn should include its own map. We would then have
>
> the map
> the map of the map
> the map of the map-of-the-map
>
> Imagine a novel that includes the novel of itself plus the novel of this novel of itself. (*O arquipélago,* 2:400)

Chaves attributes this "loss of the idea of centrality" to the Huxleyan influence (*Realismo e sociedade,* 17). At the same time, Veríssimo read such philosophers of language as Wittgenstein, to whom he alludes in the imaginary interview that prefaces the isolated edition of *Ana Terra.*[9]

Be that as it may, *O tempo e o vento* is a decentered, polymorphous novel in which different voices circulate. Dialogical. In this, fundamentally, resides its modernity. Also, in this is the greatest difference between this monumental mosaic and the prose fiction of the 1930s, which is normally turned toward the past and silenced by monologism.

The necessity to uncover the authoritarian and conservative penumbra that shadows Modernism, generally seen as rupture and innovation, is increasingly urgent. Equivalent to a period of *transition,* Modernism could not escape from the contradictions, and Brazilian modernization could not avoid its retrograde and outmoded features. Thus the importance of Veríssimo's modernity, with *O tempo e o vento,* map of the map-of-the-map, novel of this novel-of-itself. In contrast to so many novels and the majority of writers of the second modernist generation and beyond, Veríssimo, despite the lack of concision or any other reservations one might have,[10] diagnosed the Brazilian *transition,* slicing through its painful paradoxes in an acutely modern fictional incision. Because, according to the wisdom of Tio Bicho, "nobody makes omelettes without breaking eggs" (*O arquipélago,* 3:745). Or, to be more explicit, one is not modern without stepping deeply into the territory of modernity—this map-of-the-map-of-the-map, an endless abyss in which "we never stop falling."

Clasp

It is not my intention to conclude the reflections sown throughout this essay. To the contrary, I prefer to leave them open to dialogue, replies, debates, and further explorations. I cannot avoid, however, recapitulating some of the central topics discussed earlier.

Commenting on my *A permanência do círculo,* Antonio Dimas asked the following: "Isn't it natural that the contemporary Brazilian novel has changed only epidermically since our power structure has never undergone a radical transformation, but rather mere surface rearrangements?" (18).[1] I believe the answer to his question was already to be found in that study, but perhaps not explained with the clarity I had supposed.

This book no doubt reiterates the thesis developed on that occasion: from the nineteenth century until the 1930s (and with subsequent resonances), Brazilian literature—at least a significant part of it—is enclosed in a *narrow circle* which is seignorial, patriarchal, and masculine, reduplicating the values of the established order, at the service of the ruling agrarian classes' hegemony; when they decline, fiction more often than not searches for a temps perdu, struggling to restore, through recourse to memory or myth, the seignorial scene in the imaginary space of literary representation.

According to the reading undertaken here, the work of Alencar exemplifies, from the hierarchical relations between characters to the closed conception of his novelistic technique, the full force of oligarchical values in the nineteenth-century narrative. In the third decade of this century, the study emphasized, in the work of José Lins do Rego, the notion of impotence, mixed with sexual deviations, in the face of social transformation that assails the fictitious agents in an erroneous sublimation of the loss of political prestige with erotic violence. In Galeão Coutinho I attempted to stress the failure to express difference, despite the fact that he is a predominantly urban novelist, since the nostalgic aspect ultimately prevails, revealing just how much the rural heritage weighs on the city in a process of expansion. The work of both Galeão Coutinho and José Lins do Rego turns toward the past and laments, in the final analysis, the twilight of the patriarchy, the sugar aristocracy, and the coffee barons. This nostalgic gaze dispenses with any critical relationship with what was left behind, presenting, rather, a repetitive eternal return of the same.

A more complex figure such as Graciliano Ramos tends to touch on central aspects of the Brazilian *transition* (see *São Bernardo*).[2] But, as I attempted to show in *Memórias do cárcere,* his thought still owes much to what one might call a *seignorial episteme.*

For a more global but still not exhaustive vision of the situation, one should add the "intimist" novels (Cyro dos Anjos, Lúcio Cardoso, Cornélio Penna, Octávio de Faria) and the pamphletary phase of Jorge Amado, with the teleological hope for a future without bosses or employees, without misery or exploitation. I have dealt with some of the former elsewhere.[3] In the case of Jorge Amado, whom I did not discuss, literature escapes from the present by betting on the future, in a posture typical of Brazilian cultural discourse, frequently avoiding a duel with History. In general terms, if one could write that in the 1930s Brazil produced an anachronistic and backward-looking discourse, of an "aristocracy" somehow without a place in the changes the country was undergoing, in the 1950s and even later we will have a discourse, generated by the military and the entrepreneurial bourgeoisie, that ignores the past and prophesies a promising future for the nation. If the assumption is plausible, the great gap in both discursive models is a confrontation with the present in the heat of social practices, thus avoiding the risks of *moving in History.*

By no means am I advocating scorn of the past and of tradition, nor a silencing of memory. My reflections follow closely some opportune reminders of Ulpiano Bezerra de Menezes: to dominate the past, he asserts, evoking Hobsbawn, is not synonymous with social immobility (as it appears to be in the novelists of the 1930s). Human beings, immersed in the social, in the framework of historical consciousness, perceive themselves to be products of forces in action and subject to change; far from submissively assimilating the past as something weak and homogenized, they create with it a dynamic equilibrium (and an unstable one, I would add) transformed into an interlocutor which critically interrogates it. In these parameters, he proceeds, "to exile memory in the past is to cease to understand it as a living force in the present. Without memory there is no human present, nor future. Said another way: memory revolves around a basic fact of the human phenomenon, change." Or, "memory interests me because I am alive, here and now." Thus characterized, memory "has to do with history conceived not as knowledge of man in the past, but as knowledge of man's temporal dimension" (185).

Although the suspension of historical flux and neglect of the present appear to a greater or lesser degree in the texts of the authors examined here, it was primarily in the essay on Drummond that I attempted to stress the freezing of History, turned into remorse, after the effort to stifle the "bad smell of memory" that one detects in the poet's work. Paraphrasing Wander Melo Miranda, refuge in the mythical paternal house of childhood blurs interaction between past and present, since bringing the former to the surface numbs the crystalline unfolding of the latter. The detour undertaken by Drummond's memorialistic writing, turning toward an inventory of the clan, stores in a kind of limbo the commitments assumed by the writer as a public servant in the bureaucratic offices of the Estado Novo and as witness to one of the most agitated and violent periods of recent Brazilian life, between 1968 and 1979, when he published the series *Boitempo,* bringing together his poetic remembrances (10). In analogous fashion, other strategic and providential "forgettings" appear in the literature of other modernists, in whose production the recovery of the past or prognoses for the future deflect the positions taken in the agitated moment lived by the country in the 1930s.

* * *

What one concludes is that intellectuals abdicated their oppositional potential. In Humberto de Campos I attempted to underline the self-attributed function of condottieri, which is gradually frustrated by the adoption of a savage form of capitalism. A *sociology of intellectual life* would show how much the Brazilian intelligentsia closed ranks with the dominant elites in the conception and construction of an authoritarian and centralized State. On the other hand, a less indulgent approach to Modernism should consider the shifting ideological atmosphere in which it moved, rethinking the accepted interpretation that focuses on the notion of "rupture" and analyzing its discursive historicity in more depth.

As a whole, I do not see the literature of the 1930s as transgressive. The country was experiencing a *transition*, in the name of "modernization," and literary texts frequently turned toward the past or promised the future, abdicating an acute problematization of the present. In this sense, it is fundamental to pursue the hypothesis raised in this book, notably with respect to modernist poetry: the existence, as textual inscription, of an *absence of History* in the Brazilian literary and cultural discourse.

A reservation could be made, and quite correctly, that by focusing on fictional texts I have examined just one educated social segment, because it is well known that books in Brazil are luxury items enjoyed by a small minority of the population. To suggest the validity of the suspicion, I would recall that in the area of contemporary popular music we also find immobility and a lack of historical praxis, as Walnice Nogueira Galvão has argued in relation to song lyrics that mythify the "day that will come" or the song itself in her ideological analysis of Brazilian Popular Music (MPB). Examining compositions by Geraldo Vandré, Edu Lobo, Chico Buarque de Holanda, Caetano Veloso, and Gilberto Gil, she emphasized how, in them, man is not constituted as a subject of History, paradoxically preaching (since many were considered songs of protest against the military dictatorship) inaction and passiveness: "The songs of MPB result, therefore, in an evasion of the personal implications of each one in history" (Galvão, "MMPB: uma análise ideológica," 104). Even considering the later production of some of these singers and composers (Walnice's text dates from 1968), what deserves emphasis is that the contradictions detected throughout this essay reverberate in other cultural manifestations, casting serious doubt on the intervention of the Brazilian intellectual even in the recent past. And to aggravate matters, one should note that the record has a penetration and level of sales much higher than the book. This receptivity would contribute to confirm the argument's breadth.

One might further note that composers such as Chico Buarque still occupy a middle-class ideological position, not very different from that of the writers examined here. Curiously, however, an anthropological study of the theme-sambas of Carioca carnival parades—and in this case we are dealing with more popular classes—stresses that

> the (nostalgic) idealization of the past corresponds to the (hopeful or over-optimistic) idealization of the future. Both are positively valorized. The absence of the theme of the present (and present events) seems to indicate that it is valorized negatively through the contrast with a *before* and an *after* which are utopically affirmed and whose *historical veracity* cannot be judged. This would not occur with themes concerning the present. The immediate unverifiability reinforces opinions about facts which are distant in time and corroborates the ideological functions attributed to them in the expressional universe of the samba composers. (Neves, 61)

If the thesis is correct, it would be important to add to the Brazilian social dilemma, which Roberto DaMatta has studied in depth, this horror of History, which, everything leads us to believe, pervades our social formation. Avoiding a direct confrontation with the present, turning toward the past or projecting into the future—without realizing that the three dimensions are confused or that the future is constructed starting from the present—Brazilian cultural discourse relapses in the creation of notions such as "nationality," mythifying them with an atemporal aura. Basic questions, such as those of violence or dependency, are deferred, camouflaged by the barriers of ahistorical thought, which ratified the domination of power elites. A brief visit to the ideology generated by the Escola Superior de Guerra (Higher War College), the founder of the doctrine of "National Security" which patronized the country in the post-1964 regime, would be sufficient to prove the persistence of the posture described in the Brazilian scenario.

* * *

The texts and authors analyzed have led us to put in parentheses the concept of Modernism, the modernization of the country, which is so contradictory, and the idea of modernity. Among the writers of the 1930s examined here, Érico Veríssimo, notwithstanding his liberalism, which emanated from the Gaúcho patriarchy, and despite his similarities with the literary models of his time, is the writer who puts in circulation, especially in the final volume of *O tempo e o vento,* conflicting versions of events, revealing a more contemporary conception of the play of meaning and a debate involving the various positions originating in some of the thorniest years of the *transition* during the Vargas period. Curiously, I see in Machado de Assis our first viscerally modern novelist, anticipating a modernity that will be consummated in the 1940s, when novelists such as Clarice Lispector and Guimarães Rosa and poets such as João Cabral de Melo Neto explore the depths of language and make it permeable to the presence of History. Because language is History, since it permits social interaction.

The literature of the period of *transition,* in its general contours, is not modern not only because it does not venture an abyssal "map-of-the-map-of-the-map," as suggested in a passage that reveals the thoughts of Floriano, the alter ego of the Gaúcho novelist in *O arquipélago.* It is not modern because it presents a monolithic vision—that of agrarian segments—because it always narrates the same story—that segment's decadence—and because it does not admit other voices in the narrative texture. It is, in this sense, an authoritarian discourse that never permits the perspective of the other.

As a consequence, it is imperative to review the canonization of the Brazilian literary corpus, recovering discredited authors, works, and genres from ostracism. And, to escape from the elitist circuit of "serious" literature, which provides only a partial portrait of the country's social reality, it becomes urgent to weigh other, "nonliterary" cultural manifestations, in order to sound out the words of less-privileged classes who do not have access to an erudite vehicle such as the book or a "higher" art form such as literature. Not having undertaken such an enterprise in this essay, I can only reiterate its urgency.

A *way of reading* anchored in a sociocritical posture reveals the complicity of many literary texts with the project of the solidification of an authoritarian State. In effect, a cut in the Brazilian cultural discourse would explain how much its different strata—literary, philosophical, scientific, economic, political, ideological—are organized primarily around the same vector from the mid-nineteenth century until after 1964: to constitute, at any price, a modern, technocratic State in Brazil. This study has thus attempted to contribute to a cartography of discursive practices, in such a way that one may map the Brazilian social formation in its authoritarian and conservative features.

An approach along these lines would historically reorder the Brazilian literary corpus. Outlined here, such an interpretive gesture has shown how it, at least in the authors studied, encompasses a monotonous repetition of the same, without permitting differences, walking hand-in-hand with the authoritarianism of the ruling classes, a detail that seems beyond the reach of an aesthetic approach, which registers epidermic nuances by stressing criteria of "period styles." I am proposing the category of *transition* (which I attempted to elaborate theoretically in the initial chapter, but which I still recognize as porous), understanding it in its ambiguous and problematic features as capable of being used, at least strategically, to take in the period between 1850 and 1950. With no pretensions of doing so exhaustively, this essay hopes to move toward its *archaeology,* distilling a History rooted in discourse, but purposely fragmented and full of gaps.

* * *

In that lapse of time, the country engaged in a process of modernization, which occurs in a paradoxical manner, whose most accomplished political translation is summarized in the pact of 1930 and in the subsequent Vargas period. The intellectuals egressed from the decadent rural sectors still enjoy power, participating in the cultural policy of the Estado Novo. The decade's literature is basically conceived by these same intellectuals.

The absence of History in a good part of the literary production of the *transition* is not manifested only on the level of a lack of questioning about the present. We must also register its social roots. The intellectuals co-opted by the pact of 1930 searched for a new form of insertion in the institutional situation. A nebulous tenor is characteristic of the *transition,* while the new main actors are not fully cognizant of the functions to be fulfilled. The urban middle sectors are not ready; the military are in waiting; the industrialists have not yet taken control of the State apparatus; the large landowners have not yet completely left the scene.

If these intellectuals were to deal with the present and strongly to embrace History, they would be declaring, in the space of literary representation, their own death penalty, since their class fraction was being put to the test in historical reality. If History in fact flogged them, fiction was one of the doors that opened in their attempt to restore, at least in the imagination, some relics of the agonizing seignorial past. One thus understands the significant memorialistic substratum of this literary legacy. "Musketeers without a mission," they were left to be "novelists of antique shops," to recall two borrowed metaphors evoked in this book. To thematize the past (or predict the future) throws a smoke screen on the present, which tends to be justified by returning to the origins, obeying an ideological necessity of this group, which, through the reconstruction of its genealogy, attempts to explain its current domination. In accordance with this enterprise, one witnesses, on the political front, alliances with power, adhesion to Integralism and the Catholic right, flirtations with the Communist Party, service to the Capanema ministry or DIP, during the Estado Novo. Obviously, in the face of so much co-optation and alignment with order, and a literary project that is so authoritarian and restrictive of differences, we would not be justified in qualifying this literature as transgressive. To transgress, in the final analysis, would be a suicidal gesture; to collaborate, in their minds, seems to be more cautious and appropriate.

A topic that demands a more complete analysis concerns the relations between the modernist elite and power.[4] Agrarian origins underlie the biographies of a great number of the period's writers. The decline of classes linked to agricultural exports removes from their hands the capacity to dictate the rules of the political chessboard, which in some way they held while their social group manipulated power in the Old Republic. The Estado Novo will take the responsibility for integrating culture and politics: having been co-opted, this lettered minority will figure among the select ranks who adulated Vargas, having indubitably participated in the Estado Novo's "modernizing" project. Seen from this angle, notes Randal Johnson, Modernism was institutionalized with the Estado Novo dictatorship: it became "official" and canonical ("Carta," 1).[5] Intellectuals were, in fact, to a great extent responsible for Vargas's cultural policy, having collaborated in the implementation of a "modernizing" and centralizing status quo.

Little by little, however, the option made by the country, under the influence of foreign multinationals, will be for capitalist development, and there intellectuals probably have little to say.[6] In a late echo of a very romantic problematic, literary creation has few functions when what matters is putting the country on the road to modernity. Intellectuals who collaborated with the Estado Novo were bureaucrats who, taking advantage of the posts that the situation provided them, perpetuated elite dominance and contributed to cement the authoritarian framework of our cultural discourse.[7]

Again, there appears the question of the intellectual in a society such as that of Brazil. Silviano Santiago argues that the intellectual is impotent in the face of the historical process and that, unable to command it, he can only thematize the conflict in his work: "History, in which the intellectual participates as a man, is a game about which he can only be critical" ("Mesa-redonda," 436–37). What seems to have happened is that a large portion of Brazilian literature in the period of *transition,* and even afterward, has refused to confront directly the crucial questions for a precise understanding of Brazil's complexity: at the end of the century, family and race; in the 1930s, property and colonelism; in the recent 1970s, dependency and, in sum, Brazil. The answer to such burning questions, according to Flora Süssekind, assumes the form of various *band-aids* applied by ideology (in her perspective, naturalist ideology) (Süssekind, *Tal Brasil, qual romance?* 194, 173–74), covering the exposed wounds of a peripheral and underdeveloped country without identity, which has paid the price of the economic "miracle" with the interest of its foreign debt, only to achieve the dubious distinction of being the world's eighth economic power and the country with the largest imbalance in the distribution of income in the world.

A transgressive literature does not suppress social interdictions—man is a social animal and life in society demands interdictions—but, undermining them, it keeps them transgressed. "The existence of the Law makes its transgression possible" (Coelho, lxix, lxviii). Perhaps the best illustration is an example taken from another society, such as that of the Guaiaquis.

Pierre Clastres has analyzed how, among these Indians, there exists a fundamental distinction separating men and women, crystallized in the opposition between the bow and the basket, the latter extended to the women's lament, which always intones their song in chorus, and that of the men, which is nocturnal and protagonized by soloists. Guaiaqui men are forced to accept polyandry because of the excess of men and the scarcity of women. Also, hunters never eat the meat of their own prey, invariably donating their game to other members of the village.

What interests me is that the men's nocturnal chant is a means of transgressing the social interdiction to which they are obliged to conform, so that the survival of the tribe as a group will be viable. It is only in their nocturnal song that "they can articulate an experience without which they might not be able to tolerate the permanent tension that the necessities of social life impose on their daily life" (85). Clastres concludes by saying that the desire to "abolish the human condition"—perhaps the supreme transgression—and the impossibility of doing so, ends up dissolving in the space of language, where it finally comes about: "If the proximity between dream and word marks the failure of men in renouncing what they are, it also marks the triumph of language. Only in it can truth fulfill the double mission of reuniting men and breaking the ties that unite them. The only possibility for them to transcend their condition, language becomes their *beyond,* and because of their *worth,* the words said are the native land of the gods" (88).

When such considerations are transplanted to the corpus that has been the object of this book, one deduces that it is impractical to realize a powerfully transgressive literature without proceeding to a radical problematization of language and without deeply excavating History. Turning again to Marilena Chauí, a society is only historical if it occurs as time, if it reconstitutes itself at every moment, if it ceaselessly questions its genesis and its form. A society is only historical if it lives with its conflicts and accepts its differences, a society for which power is permanently in check, a society that impedes the permanence of the identical image. A society open to the plural, ready to dare "the risks of History" (*Cultura e democracia,* 103).

Minneapolis,
March 1989
(Revised—Brooklyn Park,
November 1990)

Notes

The Mask and the Face

1. See Roberto Reis, "Por uma teoria da leitura"; "Ler/dialogar—notas por uma teoria da leitura"; "A leitura como diálogo"; "O lugar da crítica e a crítica do lugar"; "Tecendo a leitura"; "Por uma crítica mestiça"; "Para uma sóciocrítica ou pedagogia da crítica."

2. Chauí thus recognizes, in Brazil's social formation, a lack of distinction between public and private; a lack of equality under the law; racial, sex, and class discrimination; a strongly hierarchical social structure; a State seen as the founder of the social order; social relations characterized by tutelage and favor. Or as she puts it: "It is a society in which social differences and asymmetries are quickly turned into inequalities, inequalities into hierarchical relations, command and obedience (a situation that goes from the family to the State, traverses public and private institutions, permeates culture and interpersonal relations). Individuals are immediately distributed in superiors and inferiors, although someone who is superior in one relationship may become inferior in another, depending on the codes of hierarchization that regulate social and personal relations. All relationships take the form of dependency, tutelage, concession, of authority and favor, making symbolic violence the rule of social and cultural life. A violence which is all the greater since it is invisible beneath paternalism and clientelism, which are considered natural and, at times, exalted as positive qualities of the 'national character'" (*Conformismo e resistência*, 54).

3. See especially the first chapter of Reis, *A permanência do círculo*.

4. Roberto Schwarz, "Nacional por subtração," in *Que horas são?* 29–48.

5. The advent of the sciences in Brazil coincided with "the ascension of the bourgeoisie and the predominance of the urban spirit over the mentality linked to the dominance of rural sectors" (Candido, "O método crítico de Sílvio Romero," 125).

6. Flora Süssekind writes that "the favorable reception of the naturalist school and scientism corresponded to the accelerated growth of an urban petite bourgeoisie, in opposition to the until then exclusive power of the 'territorial class.' Naturalism and scientism thus served as a language for a

social sector in search of greater political and cultural influence, in the midst of the social transformations underway in the country" (*Tal Brasil, qual romance?* 59). In this passage, she alludes to a work by Nelson Werneck Sodré on naturalism in Brazil.

7. "Hygienic pragmatism intuited that not everyone could continue being fathers and owners of their sons. To those who were unable to preserve the two functions there remained that of father. The agrarian State needed only a few bosses in command, but many 'fathers' to serve it. The period in which all men gave themselves the right to be both fathers and bosses was over. Hygienics revoked the pretense by showing the disasters it caused. The rights of the State argued for the rights of sons. The new child demanded a couple which, instead of behaving as property owners, accepted as a priority the role of tutor. Tutor of children whose true proprietor was the nation, the country" (Costa, *Ordem médica e norma familiar,* 170). "Brazilian society idealized by the hygienists would be composed of these strong men who, accompanied closely by doctors from birth, would one day be ready to meekly offer their lives to the country" (179).

8. "The biological hierarchy of races succeeded, in the republican regime, the blood-line hierarchy of nobility in order to perpetuate social inequalities"; "the rationale of these intellectuals [of the first three decades of the twentieth-century] is summed up in a postulate: as long as the Brazilian is not white, he has no right to democracy. This warning, among other consequences, should induce blacks and mestizos to attempt to whiten their skin and whites, both poor and rich, to exercise repression under the pretext of defending democracy" (Costa, *História da psiquiatria no Brasil,* 37).

9. Brazil still has a colonial economy, "which does not have its own center of growth, autonomy, or internal decision-making power. It is a reflexive economy that grows or declines as a result of decisions made elsewhere, controlled by its economic and financial dependency" (Iglésias, *História e ideologia,* 85). The notion is also found in Caio Prado, Jr., *História econômica do Brasil* (287–356).

10. Octávio Ianni prefers to date the urbanization of Brazilian society to around 1940, when industrialization effectively occurs, referring to the lapse of time prior to that date as a "bourgeois, city style of life" (168).

11. This attitude persists in the Brazilian social formation, assuming, for example, the variant of the famous "Do you know who you're talking to?" studied by Roberto DaMatta in chapter 4 of *Carnavais, malandros e heróis.* DaMatta notes that such expressions are used when the traditional symbols that indicated the hierarchically superior social position of an individual, such as the use of morning coats, canes, graduation rings, and fountain pens in jacket pockets, had tended to disappear (153–54).

12. "In Brazilian cities, spatial (and social) demarcation always occurs in the sense of a gradation or hierarchy between center and periphery, inside and outside. To verify this, it is sufficient to examine the expression 'center of the city,' and also the highly negative connotation of the suburban space—suburban" (DaMatta, *A casa e a rua,* 27).

13. According to DaMatta, populism "has a clear kinship component, which is closely linked to the hierarchization of the public world in terms of the private world, the home and the family" (*Carnavais,* 187).

14. On Modernism, see Mário da Silva Brito, *Antecedentes da Semana de Arte Moderna;* Antonio Candido, *Literatura e sociedade;* Wilson Martins, *A literatura brasileira—Modernismo;* Alfredo Bosi, *História concisa da literatura brasileira;* Gilberto Mendonça Teles, *Vanguarda européia e Modernismo brasileiro;* Affonso Ávila, ed., *O Modernismo* (especially the chapters by Francisco Iglésias and Benedito Nunes); João Alexandre Barbosa, "Linguagem e realidade do Modernismo de 22"; Lucia Helena, *Modernismo brasileiro e vanguarda;* João Luiz Lafetá, *1930: a crítica e o Modernismo;* João Hernesto Weber, *Do Modernismo à nova narrativa;* Silviano Santiago, "Vale quanto pesa;" Antônio Arnoni Prado, *1922—itinerário de uma falsa vanguarda;* Randal Johnson, "Brazilian Modernism: The Politics of Cultural Nationalism"; and the essays by João Alexandre Barbosa and Silviano Santiago in *O livro do seminário,* ed. Domício Proença Filho.

15. This aspect will not be discussed in depth here. I examine the question further in a study titled "Fogos de artifício."

16. On the ideology of the Brazilian intelligentsia see Dante Moreira Leite, *O caráter nacional brasileiro;* Francisco Iglésias, *História e ideologia;* A. L. Machado Neto, *Estrutura social da República das Letras;* Brito Broca, *A vida literária no Brasil—1900;* Caio Navarro de Toledo, *ISEB: fábrica de ideologias;* Gilberto Vasconcelos, *A ideologia curupira;* Bolivar Lamounier, "Formação de um pensamento autoritário na Primeira República. Uma interpretação"; Sérgio Miceli, *Poder, sexo e letras na República Velha* and *Intelectuais e classe dirigente no Brasil—1920–1945;* Jarbas Medeiros, *Ideologia autoritária no Brasil (1930–1945);* Carlos Guilherme Mota, *Ideologia da cultura brasileira (1933–1974);* Hélgio Trindade, "Integralismo: teoria e práxis política nos anos 30"; Nicolau Sevcenko, *Literatura como missão;* Reginaldo Moraes et al., ed., *Inteligência brasileira.*

17. Jarbas Medeiros writes that Azevedo Amaral's concept of social classes is contaminated by racism and elitism. For Amaral, healthy revolutions are undertaken by elites, while popular, mass movements are qualified as riots, with a pejorative connotation. Within this line of thought, revolutions, when they are "real," are essentially conservative, while riots "are always the result of the 'disorder' characteristic of the masses." One recognizes in this statement the ideology of the "pacific nature of the Brazilian people." Amaral also uses the criterion of race to

"explain the 'inviability' of democracy in our country and to support the necessity of oligarchies and elites" (Medeiros, 89).

18. Two additional examples: "When [blacks are] subjected to the discipline of the shanties, slaveholders keep them within certain customs of morality and sociability which assimilates them, as much as possible, to the superior race; however, from the moment after slavery is abolished when they are left en masse to their own direction, they decline and progressively arrive at the bastardized situation in which we see them today" (Medeiros, 190); "courageous, brave, and proud, our yokels only do well when they are under the direction of a boss, who they obey with the passivity of a perfect automaton" (192). Oliveira Vianna's thought thus proceeds by submitting diverse minorities to the yoke of the aryan elite.

19. According to Renato Ortiz, Gilberto Freyre attends to the demands of a State that was attempting to cement its social development, thus the need to overcome obsolete racial theories and propose another interpretation of Brazil. Freyre's thought, produced outside of the university (and in this resides, according to Ortiz, a great difference in relation to other social scientists such as Sérgio Buarque de Holanda and Caio Prado, Jr.), is the apex of a genealogy of intellectuals that had begun in the previous century (40).

20. "Works such as *The Masters and the Slaves* [Freyre], produced by a son of the Old Republic, indicated efforts to understand Brazilian reality undertaken by an aristocratically-oriented elite that was losing power. Corresponding to the loss of political and social strength is a revision in search of a lost time. A return to the roots. [. . .] Works such as this lofty interpretation of Brazil, produced by an essayistic tendency, in truth *conceal,* under 'regionalist' and/or 'universalist' formulas, the real problem, which is the relations of domination in Brazil" (Mota, 58–59). According to the same author, Gilberto Freyre's generation expressed the concerns of the dominant class, albeit in crisis: "It carries with it a certain sense of command, the marks of distinction and prestige, a seignorial vision of the world" (54), repeated in the period's fiction (as, for example, in José Lins do Rego); see also, for a critique of Gilberto Freyre, Dante Moreira Leite, *O caráter nacional brasileiro,* and Roberto Reis, "O coágulo e a nebulosa." Interestingly, Freyre's work also conferred importance on the quotidian as a crucial element for historical reconstruction, a characteristic which anticipated recent tendencies of historiography.

21. "The traditionalist or the restorer ignores or seeks to negate that there is a process that leads to permanent change; he sees reality in an idyllic, perfect, and beautiful manner, as something that should not be altered. Refusing to accept or not recognizing movement, he thinks in

terms of a philosophy that he supposes eternal, free from time and the environment. Since the reality that he is forced to live is not the same as the one he idealized, it condemns it as a mistake, a deviation from the truth, man's madness. And he begins to combat it, in order to restore that which he feels is correct. For him, pretensions of equality are absurd, since men are naturally unequal; there thus exists a hierarchy, with each one having different attributes, in a society in which some command and the others obey. Movements for freedom seem to him to be not only dangerous, but also false, fruit of a contaminated perspective, seen as libertine or liberticide rather than libertarian. The ideology of order is conservative, it seeks to perpetuate a state of things that seems to enclose the entire truth; since the world in which it exists no longer provides this situation, it is reactionary, it struggles against this world, it wants to return to the past. There is a paradox in the case: in the cult of tradition, of the elements that informed the process of a culture, or a people, or a nation, the ideology turns toward history, to which it attributes a frequently absolute value; not recognizing change, however, in this static vision, it is anti-historical. Traditionalism is romantic and false; in the supposition of an eternal and immutable truth, it is anti-historical, since it does not allow flux, which is the very essence of history" (Iglésias, *História e ideologia*, 112–13).

22. "There does not exist, in this sense, a Brazilian Culture on the ontological plane, but rather in the sphere of the ideological formations of highly elitist segments of the population, having acted to dissolve real contradictions. 'Racial democracy,' 'non-violent history,' etc., are easily transformed into the currency of this 'culture.' A systematic absence of studies of important social movements (Farroupilha; Balaiada; 1930) and significant ideological lineages indicate an exemplary omission in relation to the central themes that should mark the framework of this culture" (Mota, 269).

23. Even Oswald and Graciliano have been the object of analyses that point out enormous contradictions. On Oswald, see Randal Johnson, "Modernism and Authoritarianism in Brazil," and Leslie Bary, "Civilization, Barbarism, Cannibalism: Self and Other in Oswald de Andrade." On Graciliano, see Lamberto Puccinelli, *Graciliano Ramos;* Lúcia Helena Carvalho, *A ponta do novelo;* and José Carlos Garbuglio et al., ed., *Graciliano Ramos.*

24. Consuelo Albergaria's article, in my opinion, does not explore this vein in Rosa to the ultimate consequences. Few studies of his work with a social orientation exist, such as that of Walnice Nogueira Galvão, *As formas do falso,* and Roberto DaMatta's analysis of "A hora e vez de Augusto Matraga" in *Carnavais, malandros e heróis.*

The Self-Portrait and the Back of the Portrait

1. The first number in parentheses refers to the original Portuguese version, listed in the bibliography, and the second to the English translation, "The Psychiatrist," trans. William L. Grossman and Helen Caldwell. The Portuguese word 'alienista' has been rendered as 'alienist' rather than the 'psychiatrist' of the Goodman-Caldwell translation [translator's note].

2. 'Canjica,' in Portuguese, is formed from the root 'canja,' meaning 'chicken soup,' and the diminutive suffix '-ica.' The term also refers to a dish made with grated green corn, sugar, coconut milk, and cinnamon or to a cyst in the flesh of swine [translator's note].

3. At least two books published after this chapter was written would be important for the discussion undertaken here: Flora Süssekind's *O Brasil não é longe daqui* and Roberto Schwarz's *Um mestre na periferia do capitalismo.*

The Carpenter of Letters

1. I allude here, not without irony, to the fact that the Republic was not brought about by a popular movement that substantially altered the country's social structure. Certainly, from a historical perspective, the proclamation of the Republic was a much more complex phenomenon than is revealed in the fact of having been crowned by the protest mentioned. For an excellent interpretation of the period's underlying social dynamic, I recommend Décio Saes, *Classe média e política na Primeira República.*

2. The same happened in São Paulo, which ceased being a concentrated city where workers lived in the center close to the elites, paying rent in slums and boardinghouses, to become a dispersed and segregated city in which workers live in their own self-constructed houses in peripheral, outlying areas. That is, there occurred a process of expulsion of low-income workers to distant neighborhoods which were accessible economically only because they did not have an adequate infrastructure or network of basic services. In other words, with population growth and the decrease in the supply of housing, low-income workers could only "live in the sticks" (Caldeira, 17).

3. I borrowed heavily from Sevcenko's *Literatura como missão* when writing this section.

4. It would be interesting to relate this process of political, cultural, and urban purification with the attempt undertaken by hygienic medicine to carry out an asepsis in the Brazilian family. See Jurandir Freire Costa (*Ordem médica e norma familiar*) and Katia Muricy (especially 21–32).

5. I allude here to a passage in the epilogue of Mário de Andrade's *Macunaíma.* I explored the metaphor in the essay "A fala impura."

6. It would be worthwhile to compare this with Lúcia Miguel-Pereira's analysis of Coelho Neto (260–69). On the period, see also Bosi, *O Pré-Modernismo,* and Jeffrey Needell, *A Tropical Belle Époque,* which I read after this chapter was written.

The Almond Tree and the Banana

1. The first number in parentheses refers to the original Portuguese version, listed in the bibliography, the second to the English translation. See *Plantation Boy,* trans. Emmi Baum [translator's note].

2. The best study of *Fogo morto* that I am aware of is by Heloísa Toller Gomes. The essay by José Sérgio Leite Lopes, which deals with the patriarchal family, is also worth consulting. Both, along with others, are listed in the bibliography.

3. Compare this opinion with the following passage: "Only in *Bangüê* will the consciousness of exploitation appear, and even there it will not go beyond pity. In the lower classes there is no class consciousness. In the upper classes the feeling is more of kinship than of class" (Pacheco, 16). This notation coincides with the structure of colonelistic society, as studied by Maria Isaura Pereira de Queiroz in *O mandonismo local na vida política brasileira.*

4. About Vitorino, Heloísa Toller Gomes writes: "The only example [. . .] of a character who thinks he undertakes effective social action is that of Vitorino Carneiro da Cunha. Vitorino is a curious (and inviable) synthesis of landowner and poor white: zealous of tradition and lineage like the former (with whom he is connected by family ties), destitute of property and of a defined position in the mechanism like the latter, he thinks he moves freely among the dominant and the dominated, ignoring the rigidity of dividing lines between social positions. Besides [. . .] the question of decadence never occurs to him, and he prepares for the future with optimism in a decrepit society. Despite his provocative and irreverent language, Vitorino is paradoxically the character who believes in the regime's efficacy. But the discourse of *Fogo morto* signals the world of fantasy in which Vitorino moves, and his action is totally in vain, adding nothing to the social panorama" (144).

5. In Brazilian slang, a "banana" is a cowardly weakling [translator's note].

6. Heloísa Toller Gomes also analyzes this character: the spectacular appearances of Antônio Silvino "merely mobilize the population emotionally, and are totally void of a concrete social impact. The cangaceiro appears in *Fogo morto* as an escape valve for the poor population, which

transfers its desire for power and justice to him. Part of this population, therefore, sees him as incorruptible and as an eventual liberator of the poor, instead of perceiving that, to the contrary, he is a result and integral part of the social crisis" (144).

7. Curiously, one of the best critical evaluations of Lins do Rego is in a work of "fiction." In *Em liberdade,* the false diary of Graciliano Ramos signed by Silviano Santiago, we read: "The process of social and economic disqualification of today's characters does not 'stain' their ancestors. Today's decadence does not come from the past; it is exclusively fruit of the incompetence of today's men. How does one dare touch the giants of the past? It would be a sacrilege. Past and present are separate areas within fiction" (118).

8. Brazil in the 1920s is the setting for the modernization "of the bases on which a recently republican country rested on the centennial of its political-administrative independence. Against the rural oligarchies, representatives of the agrarian structure of Brazilian society, strengthened by republican decentralization and detaining political power through their principal representatives—São Paulo and Minas Gerais—an entrepreneurial class is found whose interests are turned toward the country's industrial development, an industry that brings with it a young, conflictive and dissatisfied working class, responsible for maintaining a political climate of constant tension. But it is among young Army officers that the opposition to traditional oligarchies finds its most radicalized segments: the tenentes (lieutenants) later became a bulwark of a process of political protest that runs through the 20s and culminates in the Revolution of 1930 and the defeat of the coffee oligarchies" (Tolipan, 9).

9. The desire to kill Faria and the subsequent murder of Eurídice evoke the desire to kill the feminine character in *Bangüê.* Carlos is unable to dominate the educated Maria Alice, who awakens his lustfulness. A short passage will suffice to mark, with respect to the relationship of the protagonist-narrators with women, the novels' similarity: "Maria Alice of English novels, so well educated, so superior to me, so full of intuition and wisdom. My love for her grew as she was weakened, humiliated, and softened by the oils of lust" (80). It would be interesting in this regard to compare *Eurídice* with Graciliano Ramos's *Angústia.*

10. This detail deserves further analysis. Many character-narrators of Brazilian literature in the period of *transition*—and I think of *Dom Casmurro* and *São Bernardo*—use writing with the intent of reconstituting a power that had escaped from their control.

11. The cellmate also says the following to Julinho: truth "was hidden, disguised, to give us the surprise of convincing us, of contradicting us, of being stronger than our desires. I remained quiet, but my cellmate was ready to expose my weakness to me" (86).

12. Describing the process of composition of the urban middle sectors, Décio Saes observes that the former sugar plantation owners, like the bankrupt coffee growers of the Paraíba valley, suffered a great shock with abolition and the subsequent decline of the agro-export economy, but in a more intense manner: "Conservatism and the anxiety of maintaining social prestige were fed by a more intense nostalgia for the past, deriving from their great difficulty, relative to the social groups of the coffee growing zone, of integrating themselves acceptably in urban life" (*Classe média e política na Primeira República,* 37). Such a commentary is valid for an analysis of the narratives of Lins do Rego, and also for a study of the literature of the 1930s as a whole. The same essayist notes, in case we want to complicate the situation even more, José Lins do Rego's affiliation with Integralism (37).

The Narrow Limits

1. I cite from the first edition, in four volumes. The first volume is subtitled "Viagens," the second "Pavilhão dos Primários," the third "Colônia Correcional," and the last "Casa de Correção." The numbers in parentheses refer to the volume and the page of the citation, respectively.

2. As is well known, the Estado Novo corresponds to the dictatorship of Getúlio Vargas (1937–1945). With the so-called Intentona Comunista of 1935 there began a witch hunt, even before the dictatorship was decreed. The coup, planned since the end of 1936, merely consummated an already existing situation. I thus use the term Estado Novo to refer to the period Graciliano was imprisoned, even before its real implantation. See Edgar Carone, *O Estado Novo,* and Hélio Silva's monumental *O ciclo de Vargas,* in 16 volumes.

3. Michel Foucault, "What Is an Author?"

4. One should remember that in Brazil law is "elastic" rather than "monolithic." One example suffices: in Rio de Janeiro it is prohibited to smoke on public transportation, but people smoke and nothing happens. This "maleability," which goes against its disciplinary purpose, seems to escape Graciliano Ramos's interpretation.

5. "Graciliano's classicism resides in his extreme simplicity of means to attain an extreme complexity of ends" (Athayde, 194). For a discussion of the subject, see the "Mesa-redonda" in *Graciliano Ramos* (Garbuglio, 417–50).

6. Critics have recently focused on the contradictory positions of Graciliano Ramos, initially considered a left intellectual concerned with social problems, but who, under more careful examination, turns toward the traditional past which characterizes the Brazilian social formation at the turn of the century. Among others, see Puccinelli, especially the analysis

of the novel *São Bernardo,* and Lúcia Helena Carvalho, *A ponta do novelo,* an impeccable reading of *Angústia.*

7. In relation to nineteenth-century Brazilian fiction, I have studied how any movement of characters of the periphery ("low") toward the center of power ("high") is immediately rejected. See Reis, *A permanência do círculo.*

8. For a synthesis of Graciliano Ramos's contradictions, see Valentim Facioli's intellectual biography (especially 105).

9. Antelo suggests that besides being valuational, Graciliano Ramos's binary dialectic is also authoritarian. He cites a passage from "Quadros e costumes do nordeste" (now in *Viventes das Alagoas,* 100): "A boxer told me some time ago that society is composed of hustlers and suckers. It would be impossible to find a third grouping [. . .]. It's useless for us to want to destroy the natural order of things" (Antelo, 55).

The Pearl Necklace

1. Galeão Coutinho alludes to the Machadian influence in the preface to the second edition of *Memórias de Simão, o caolho* (10). See the bibliography for the editions of his works consulted.

2. See these examples: "after the intercostal neuralgia I acquired the sensibility of a spoiled child" (33); "Dona Marcolina is a prolongation of my mother [. . .]. She treats me with a severity that only mothers use with their loved ones for fear of losing them" (28); Dona Marcolina "took care of me like a mother takes care of a child, and a mother knows that she can't have her son close to her all her life" (106); "Dona Marcolina is a wife and a second mother" (135).

3. A work such as *Dom Casmurro* already points toward a weakening of the masculine order. See Reis, *A permanência do círculo* (88).

4. There are numerous dialogues between texts in Brazilian literature—in Machado de Assis, Autran Dourado, Murilo Rubião, Dalton Trevisan—but they do not occur in a contrastive form. If, in *Confidências,* the point of view were really that of Dona Marcolina as woman, we would have something original.

5. I call "seignorial" a *scene* dominated by the fazendeiro or the sugar-mill owner, starting from whom hierarchical relations of power are established, either with the other members of the family, with figures outside of the clan, or with the slaves. In this context ruled by seignorial values, the masculine and patriarchal order dominates, based on the preponderant figures of the man and the father.

6. The town of Barra Mansa, located in the Paraíba Valley in the state of Rio de Janeiro, was an important coffee-producing zone which entered a period of decline with Abolition.

7. It is interesting to compare the enumerations of tools used by the grandfather on the fazenda with the electrical appliances listed in the manual which starts Barra's activity as a salesman.

8. The reader will have noticed the relationship between the birds, the grandfather's closeness to nature, and the name of the fazenda where the novelist spent his childhood—"Floresta" (forest).

All History Is Remorse

1. In Murilo, "the dimension of History as a process is lost. And situated on an eternal and immutable base (the truth of Catholicism), his poetry becomes anti-historical. It believes itself to have one foot in eternity, free from time and space, when it is in fact inserted in a project of spiritualist reaction. [. . .]. A poetry about an exemplary History and rigid paradigms of language, will erect itself as a support for a Christian moral system and a (supposedly) immutable order" (Süssekind, "Murilo Mendes: um bom exemplo na História," 169).

2. See the essay by Gilda de Mello e Souza and Antonio Candido.

3. "The great theme of Vinicius's poetry is the woman. [. . .]. The woman is the great enigma of his poetry. He transfers his problems to her, he projects himself onto her, he dramatizes in her his divided self and his search for unity. In his transcendental phase, the woman he searches for is the "unique woman," the total cosmic being, the great consoling mother, a sort of Beatriz or Sophia" (Sant'Anna, *O canibalismo amoroso,* 259).

4. "It is thus notable how much Cecília Meireles's poetry imitates life as a cycle that goes from nothing to nothing, in an evolution that passes through the greatest identity with the world's values (pan-mysticism), reaches a climax (epico-lyrical expression) and then returns" (Zagury, 96).

5. David Brookshaw alludes to Jorge de Lima's hollow revindications in favor of blacks, to the falsity of his black themes, and to his profound racial prejudice (95).

6. I allude to Luiz Costa Lima's essay, published in *Cadernos da PUC.*

7. The best available source for a discussion of modernist intellectuals is Sérgio Miceli's *Intelectuais e classe dirigente no Brasil.*

8. I refer to the article by Haroldo de Campos published in *Metalinguagem.*

9. Cf. Reis, "Os dentes do poema." See also the study by Benedito Nunes. [The expression "severinidade sem plumas" refers to two long epic-dramatic poems by João Cabral de Melo Neto: "O cão sem plumas" (1950) and "Morte e vida severina" (1955); translator's note.]

10. The concrete subject here is not of interest, despite the fact that Drummond once declared that his poetry is autobiographical (Sant'Anna, *Carlos Drummond de Andrade: análise da obra,* 22).

11. Unless otherwise indicated, I will cite from the 5th edition of *Reunião,* published in 1973. [At least three volumes of Drummond's poetry have appeared in English translation: *In the Middle of the Road,* trans. John Nist; *The Minus Sign,* trans. Virginia de Araújo; and *Travelling in the Family,* ed. Thomas Colchie and Mark Strand. Although all three volumes have been consulted, translations in the text may or may not coincide with any of them. Translator's note.]

12. Here I gloss Silviano Santiago's interpretation of the poem "Infância." This essay has its beginnings in his *Carlos Drummond de Andrade.*

13. See the studies by Luiz Costa Lima in *Lira e antilira* and *Dispersa demanda.* In the latter, we read: "Corrosion is thus the central figure of Drummond's poetics. Through it there speak both the power that is eroded and the dissolution that occurs. That is, corrosion takes in both affective adherence to the space against which the poet had rebelled—his guilt—and the ruins with which he identifies—his relative freedom" (172); "coming to the present or remaining in the past, Drummond's poetics always live from what is left over" (173); "historical time, in a manner of speaking, consumes things and belongings, until there remain only leavings, which language leans over, inverting its movement of loss" (174). For Costa Lima, however, there is no nostalgic dimension in Drummond.

14. Compare this with the treatment of the same theme in the poem "Família" (["Family"], 20). Also, note the detail in the first stanza of "O enterrado vivo" (["Buried Alive"], 206): "é sempre no passado aquele orgasmo, / é sempre no presente aquele duplo, / é sempre no futuro aquele pânico"—the past connotes pleasure, the present an identity crisis, the future, fear.

15. Merquior writes: "The rebellion against the father is the source of all revolts in Drummond's verse, the original humus of his vision of the world and of society" (*Verso universo em Drummond,* 206). The most clearly memorialistic poems appear to pacify this conflictive relationship, which is "resolved" only on the poetic plane of language.

16. The feminine figure is infrequent in Drummond's poetry, which includes poems for his grandson, but none for his daughter or his wife, with his mother appearing very timidly on two occasions. Nor are there many poems that narrate amorous relations, creators of alterity, which could be understood as a principle of History to the extent that histories are fused in love. With regard to the treatment of women, if she is black, the relation is sexual and horizontal, in the Cutucum ("Ar livre" [Open Air], *Boitempo,* 54); if she is white, the relationship is spiritualized and vertical ("Orion," *Boitempo,* 89). In addition, compare "Le voyeur" (132) with "Tentativa" ([Attempt], 134), both from *Menino antigo.*

The Map of the Map-of-the-Map

1. See the editions listed in the bibliography. The initial dates of publication are: *O continente*, 1949; *O retrato*, 1951; and *O arquipélago*, 1961.

2. On Veríssimo, see the works consulted ahead. It is curious that criticism of *O tempo e o vento* tends to focus on *O continente*, the first novel of the trilogy and the one considered most successful. My reading puts more emphasis on *O arquipélago*, the trilogy's final volume.

3. "Another phenomenon is also clear in *O continente* which is inseparable from the rural patriarchy. That is the woman, who is doubly dominated. Her situation and her behavior are determined beforehand, and her fate of working and taking care of the house and waiting on her husband and children is irrepealable. It is natural for the man to have *chinocas*, or prostitutes" (Fresnot, 27).

4. In his memoirs Veríssimo narrates the episode with Cordélia, who furnishes the model for the scene that is at the origin of the conflict between Floriano and his father in *O arquipélago* (Veríssimo, *Solo de clarineta*, 1:63).

5. On Dourado's novel, see Reis, *A permanência do círculo*, chapter 4.

6. Donaldo Schüler observes that the novel's epigraph, taken from Ecclesiastes, "underlines two aspects of the work: the passing of generations and the permanence of natural phenomena." "Although time passes, the wind remains" (Chaves, ed., *O contador de histórias*, 164ff.).

7. On the mythical and ideological implications of *O continente*, Regina Zilbermann's study is elucidative (Chaves, ed., *O contador de histórias*, 176–93).

8. According to Regina Zilbermann, women represent the struggle for the preservation of a mythical and closed way of life (188–92).

9. "Just yesterday I read an astonishing citation of Wittgenstein in which this philosopher-philologist asks if there really exists some verifiable relationship between words and facts, since what we call a fact may well be just a veil woven by language to hide reality from the eyes of the spirit. [. . .] Wittgenstein asks further if we can speak of reality since speech is just a kind of infinite regression, words that are used to speak other words" (Veríssimo, "Ana Terra revisitada," xi).

10. I am thinking here of a potentially reactionary position by considering that Veríssimo's ethics attempt first to restore the collective organism, in an "exaltation of good habits" and in a praise of a "well refined family system," as Guilhermino César accentuates (Chaves, *Realismo e sociedade*, 69). José Hildebrando Dacanal is more incisive: "*O tempo e o vento* has a central axis or, better, *it is* the self-praise, simultaneously exalted and melancholic, of Rio Grande do Sul's rural patriarchy. It is the story of the

"Gaúcho" *fathers of the Nation,* told from their perspective and using a whole self-justifying mythology" (*Revista do Unificado,* 15). See also the chapter dedicated to Veríssimo in his *O romance de 30.*

Clasp

1. Professor Antônio Dimas was one member of the examining committee for my doctoral dissertation (1983), which was published with slight modifications as *A permanência do círculo.* In the passage cited, he refers to the dissertation. I do not fully understand the meaning of the adjective 'contemporary,' since my study covered the nineteenth-century novel and the second modernist moment.

2. For Silviano Santiago, Graciliano Ramos "is the only [modernist writer] who realizes that Brazilian history is false. And, since this social history is false, his characters are practically ahistorical, because they are outside of what they call History" ("Mesa-redonda," 428).

3. On Cyro dos Anjos and Lúcio Cardoso, see *A permanência do círculo,* chapters 2 and 3. On Cornélio Penna, see Luiz Costa Lima, *A perversão do trapezista;* on Octávio de Faria, consult Randal Johnson's article, "Authoritarian Fiction: Octávio de Faria's *Tragédia burguesa.*"

4. I have discussed the issue in the unpublished essay "Fogos de artifício—anotações para o estudo do sistema intelectual brasileiro."

5. I am grateful to Professor Randal Johnson for the valuable observations in this letter. For a broader exploration of the question, see his "The Dynamics of the Brazilian Literary Field, 1930–1945."

6. I am thinking here of the interpretation Décio Saes undertakes of the Brazilian middle class, alluding to the pulverization, by the political system, of its influence on the decision-making process (*Classe média e sistema político no Brasil,* 23). For him, in fact, in this there resides one of the specific features of Brazilian peripheral capitalist development: the urban middle sectors are integrated into the system of power in 1930, when the country changes from an agrarian to an industrial country and capitalism is consolidated, a process which demanded their incorporation, only to be excluded in 1964, when the political system was rearticulated due to monopoly capital's need to expand (24). Something similar occurred with intellectuals after the Vargas regime: co-optation had integrated these descendants of great patriarchal families, disqualified with the failure of sugarmills and plantations, but, once the task of giving shape to the Estado Novo's ideology through the agencies responsible for the regime's cultural facets is completed, a good portion of this intelligentsia will be gradually distanced from the decision-making nerve center, ending up without an important social role to fulfill. One notes, in this sense, how

intellectuals, during the post-1964 military regime (when the military elite will generate its own ideology, the National Security Doctrine, in the Higher War College), will be substituted by technocrats, who will take charge of drawing the new links of official policy in relation to culture, which increasingly falls under the State's tutelage (the creation of agencies such as FUNARTE, in a repetition of what had occurred during the period of the Estado Novo dictatorship).

7. This essay was already written when I had access to the studies of Luciano Martins and Mônica Pimenta Velloso, both of which are seminal for this discussion.

Bibliography

Albergaria, Consuelo. "O autor como instância de poder." Conference on Luso-Brazilian Literatures: a Socio-Critical Approach. Minneapolis, University of Minnesota, 1988.

Albuquerque, J. Guilhon de. "Ficção e realidade: o lugar das idéias." *Ensaios de Opinião* 9, 2–7 (1978): 55–57.

Alencar, José de. *O guarani*. Rio de Janeiro: Ouro, n.d.

———. *Iracema*. Rio de Janeiro: Ouro, 1967.

———. *Lucíola*. Rio de Janeiro: Ouro, n.d.

———. *Senhora*. 6th ed. São Paulo: Ática, 1975.

———. *O sertanejo*. 2d ed. São Paulo: Ática, 1977.

———. *Til*. São Paulo: Ática, 1980.

———. *Ubirajara*. Rio de Janeiro: Ouro, n.d.

Almeida, José Maurício Gomes de. *A tradição regionalista no romance brasileiro*. Rio de Janeiro: Achiamé, 1980.

Alphonsus, João. *Totônio Pacheco*. 3d ed. Rio de Janeiro: Imago, 1976.

Amado, Genolino. "Prefácio" to *Vovô Morungaba*, by Galeão Coutinho, 11–16.

Andrade, Carlos Drummond de. *Boitempo*. 2d ed. Rio de Janeiro: Sabiá, 1973.

———. *In the Middle of the Road*. Translated by John Nist. Tucson: University of Arizona Press, 1965.

———. *Menino antigo*. 3d ed. Rio de Janeiro: José Olympio, 1978.

———. *The Minus Sign*. Translated by Virginia de Araújo. Manchester: Carcanet New Press, 1981.

———. *Reunião*. 5th ed. Rio de Janeiro: José Olympio, 1973.

———. *Travelling in the Family*. Translated by Thomas Colchie and Mark Strand. New York: Random House, 1986.

Andrade, Mário de. *Macunaíma*. 6th ed. São Paulo: Martins, 1970.

———. "O movimento modernista." In *Aspectos da literatura brasileira*, 6th ed., 231–55. São Paulo: Martins, 1978.

Anjos, Cyro dos. *Abdias*. 4th ed. Porto Alegre: Globo, 1965.

———. *O amanuense Belmiro*. 9th ed. Rio de Janeiro: José Olympio, 1979.

Antelo, Raúl. *Literatura em revista*. São Paulo: Ática, 1984.

Araújo, Laís Corrêa de. *Murilo Mendes*. Petrópolis: Vozes, 1972.

Assis, Machado de. *O alienista*. 5th ed. São Paulo: Ática, 1977.

———. *The Psychiatrist and Other Stories*. Translated by William L. Grossman and Helen Caldwell. Berkeley: University of California Press, 1966.

———. *Quincas Borba*. Rio de Janeiro: Ouro, 1964.

Athayde, Tristão de. "Os ramos de Graciliano." In Posfácio a Ramos, *Viventes das Alagoas*, 191–97.

Ávila, Affonso, ed. *O Modernismo*. São Paulo: Perspectiva, 1975.

Barbosa, João Alexandre. "Linguagem e realidade do Modernismo de 22." In *A metáfora crítica*, 73–106. São Paulo: Perspectiva, 1974.

———. "A modernidade do romance." In Proença, ed., *O livro do seminário*, 19–42.

Bary, Leslie. "Civilization, Barbarism, Cannibalism: Self and Other in Oswald de Andrade." Conference on Luso-Brazilian Literatures: A Socio-Critical Approach. Minneapolis, University of Minnesota, 1988.

Bastos, Elide Rugai. "Gilberto Freyre e a questão nacional." In Moraes et al., eds., *Inteligência brasileira*, 43–76.

Bosi, Alfredo. *Céu, inferno*. São Paulo: Ática, 1988.

———. *História concisa da literatura brasileira*. 2d ed. São Paulo: Cultrix, 1976.

———. "As letras na Primeira República." In Fausto, *História geral da civilização brasileira*. tomo III, vol. 2. 293–319.

———. "A máscara e a fenda." In Alfredo Bosi et al., eds., *Machado de Assis*, 437–57. São Paulo: Ática, 1982.

———. *O Pré-Modernismo*. 5th ed. São Paulo: Cultrix, n.d.

Brito, Mário da Silva. *Antecedentes da Semana de Arte Moderna*. 2d ed. Rio de Janeiro: Civilização Brasileira, 1964.

Brito, Ronaldo. "A Semana de 22—o trauma do moderno." In Sérgio Tolipan et al., *Sete ensaios sobre o Modernismo*, 13–17. Rio de Janeiro: FUNARTE, 1983.

Broca, Brito. *A vida literária no Brasil—1900*. 3d ed. Rio de Janeiro: José Olympio, 1975.

Brookshaw, David. *Raça e cor na literatura brasileira*. Porto Alegre: Mercado Aberto, 1983.

Caldeira, Teresa Pires do Rio. *A política dos outros*. São Paulo: Brasiliense, 1984.

Campos, Haroldo de. "Lirismo e participação." In *Metalinguagem*, 79–85. Petrópolis: Vozes, 1967.

Campos, Humberto de. *Contrastes*. Rio de Janeiro: José Olympio, 1936.

———. *Crítica*, primeira série. 3d ed. Rio de Janeiro: José Olympio, 1935.

———. *Crítica*, segunda série. 2d ed. Rio de Janeiro: José Olympio, 1935.

———. *Da seara de Booz*. 2d ed. Rio de Janeiro: Jackson, 1945.

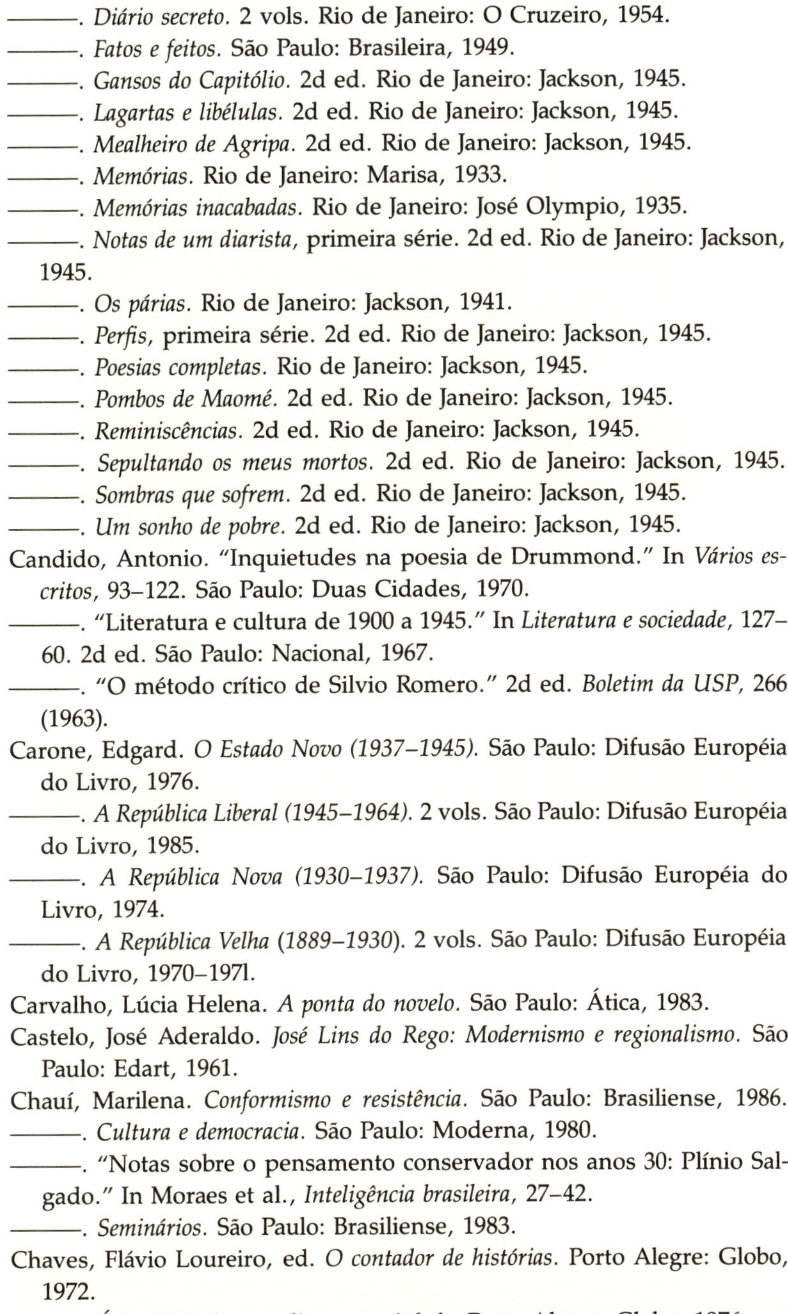

———. *Diário secreto.* 2 vols. Rio de Janeiro: O Cruzeiro, 1954.
———. *Fatos e feitos.* São Paulo: Brasileira, 1949.
———. *Gansos do Capitólio.* 2d ed. Rio de Janeiro: Jackson, 1945.
———. *Lagartas e libélulas.* 2d ed. Rio de Janeiro: Jackson, 1945.
———. *Mealheiro de Agripa.* 2d ed. Rio de Janeiro: Jackson, 1945.
———. *Memórias.* Rio de Janeiro: Marisa, 1933.
———. *Memórias inacabadas.* Rio de Janeiro: José Olympio, 1935.
———. *Notas de um diarista,* primeira série. 2d ed. Rio de Janeiro: Jackson, 1945.
———. *Os párias.* Rio de Janeiro: Jackson, 1941.
———. *Perfis,* primeira série. 2d ed. Rio de Janeiro: Jackson, 1945.
———. *Poesias completas.* Rio de Janeiro: Jackson, 1945.
———. *Pombos de Maomé.* 2d ed. Rio de Janeiro: Jackson, 1945.
———. *Reminiscências.* 2d ed. Rio de Janeiro: Jackson, 1945.
———. *Sepultando os meus mortos.* 2d ed. Rio de Janeiro: Jackson, 1945.
———. *Sombras que sofrem.* 2d ed. Rio de Janeiro: Jackson, 1945.
———. *Um sonho de pobre.* 2d ed. Rio de Janeiro: Jackson, 1945.
Candido, Antonio. "Inquietudes na poesia de Drummond." In *Vários escritos,* 93–122. São Paulo: Duas Cidades, 1970.
———. "Literatura e cultura de 1900 a 1945." In *Literatura e sociedade,* 127–60. 2d ed. São Paulo: Nacional, 1967.
———. "O método crítico de Silvio Romero." 2d ed. *Boletim da USP,* 266 (1963).
Carone, Edgard. *O Estado Novo (1937–1945).* São Paulo: Difusão Européia do Livro, 1976.
———. *A República Liberal (1945–1964).* 2 vols. São Paulo: Difusão Européia do Livro, 1985.
———. *A República Nova (1930–1937).* São Paulo: Difusão Européia do Livro, 1974.
———. *A República Velha (1889–1930).* 2 vols. São Paulo: Difusão Européia do Livro, 1970–1971.
Carvalho, Lúcia Helena. *A ponta do novelo.* São Paulo: Ática, 1983.
Castelo, José Aderaldo. *José Lins do Rego: Modernismo e regionalismo.* São Paulo: Edart, 1961.
Chauí, Marilena. *Conformismo e resistência.* São Paulo: Brasiliense, 1986.
———. *Cultura e democracia.* São Paulo: Moderna, 1980.
———. "Notas sobre o pensamento conservador nos anos 30: Plínio Salgado." In Moraes et al., *Inteligência brasileira,* 27–42.
———. *Seminários.* São Paulo: Brasiliense, 1983.
Chaves, Flávio Loureiro, ed. *O contador de histórias.* Porto Alegre: Globo, 1972.
———. *Érico Veríssimo: realismo e sociedade.* Porto Alegre: Globo, 1976.

Clastres, Pierre. "O arco e o cesto." In *A sociedade contra o Estado,* 71–89. 2d ed. Rio de Janeiro: Francisco Alves, 1982.

Coelho, Edmundo Campos. "A instituição militar no Brasil—um ensaio bibliográfico." *Boletim Informativo e Bibliográfico de Ciências Sociais* 19 (1985): 5–19.

Coelho, Eduardo Prado. "Introdução a um pensamento cruel: estruturas, estruturalidade, estruturalismos." In Coelho, ed., *Estruturalismo,* l–lxxv. Lisboa: Portugália/Martins Fontes, n.d.

Costa, Jurandir Freire. *História da psiquiatria no Brasil.* 2d ed. Rio de Janeiro: Documentário, 1976.

———. *Ordem médica e norma familiar.* 2d ed. Rio de Janeiro: Graal, 1983.

Coutinho, Eduardo, et al. *Ensaios sobre José Lins do Rego.* João Pessoa: Fundação Cultural da Paraíba, 1988.

Coutinho, Galeão. *Confidências de Dona Marcolina.* Rio de Janeiro: Ouro, n.d.

———. *Memórias de Simão, o caolho.* 5th ed. Rio de Janeiro: Civilização Brasileira, 1978.

———. *A vocação de Vitorino Lapa.* São Paulo: Martins, 1942.

———. *Vovô Morungaba.* 4th ed. Rio de Janeiro: Civilização Brasileira, 1977.

Dacanal, José Hildebrando. *Revista do Unificado* 1.1 (1978): 14–17.

———. *O romance de 30.* Porto Alegre: Mercado Aberto, 1982.

DaMatta, Roberto. *Carnavais, malandros e heróis.* Rio de Janeiro: Zahar, 1979.

———. *A casa e a rua.* São Paulo: Brasiliense, 1985.

———. *O que faz o brasil, Brasil?* Rio de Janeiro: Rocco, 1986.

Dassin, Joan. *Política e poesia em Mário de Andrade.* São Paulo: Duas Cidades, 1978.

Diégues Júnior, Manuel. "Populações rurais brasileiras." In Tamás Szmrecsányi and Oriowaldo Queda, eds., *Vida rural e mudança social,* 2d ed., 121–31. São Paulo: Nacional, 1976.

Dimas, Antonio. *Espaço e romance.* São Paulo: Ática, 1985.

Facioli, Valentim. "Um homem bruto da terra (biografia intelectual)." In Garbuglio et al., eds., *Graciliano Ramos,* 23–106.

Fausto, Boris, ed. *História geral da civilização brasileira* (O Brasil Republicano). 3 vols. São Paulo: Difusão Européia do Livro, 1975–1977.

———. "Nota introdutória." In Fausto, *História geral da civilização brasileira,* tomo III, vol. 1, 7–9.

Felizardo, Joaquim J. *História nova da República Velha.* 2d ed. Petrópolis: Vozes, 1980.

Fernandes, Florestan. *Educação e sociedade no Brasil.* São Paulo: Dominus, 1966.

———. *A revolução burguesa no Brasil.* 2d ed. Rio de Janeiro: Zahar, 1976.

Fontes, Amando. *Os Corumbas.* 13th ed. Rio de Janeiro: José Olympio, 1979.

———. *Rua do Siriri.* Rio de Janeiro: Ouro, n.d.

Foucault, Michel. *Les mots et les choses.* Paris: Gallimard, 1966.

———. "What Is an Author?" In Josué Harari, ed., *Textual Strategies: Perspectives in Post-Structuralist Criticism,* 141–60. Ithaca: Cornell University Press, 1979.

Franco, Maria Sylvia. *Homens livres na ordem escravocrata.* São Paulo: Instituto de Estudos Brasileiros, 1969.

Fresnot, Daniel. *O pensamento político de Érico Veríssimo.* Rio de Janeiro: Graal, 1977.

Fusco, Rosário. *O agressor.* 2d ed. Rio de Janeiro: Francisco Alves, 1976.

Galvão, Walnice Nogueira. *As formas do falso.* São Paulo: Perspectiva, 1972.

———. "MMPB: uma análise ideológica." In *Saco de gatos,* 93–119. São Paulo: Duas Cidades, 1976.

Garbuglio, José Carlos. "Apresentação." In Assis, *O alienista,* 5–8.

Garbuglio, José Carlos, et al., eds. *Graciliano Ramos.* São Paulo: Ática, 1987.

Gledson, John. *Poesia e poética de Carlos Drummond de Andrade.* São Paulo: Duas Cidades, 1981.

Gomes, Heloísa Töller. *O poder rural na ficção.* São Paulo: Ática, 1981.

Guimarães, Júlio Castañon. "Poesia e Pré-Modernismo." In Vários Autores, *Sobre o Pré-Modernismo,* 49–61.

Helena, Lucia. *Modernismo brasileiro e vanguarda.* São Paulo: Ática, 1986.

Holanda, Sérgio Buarque de. *Raízes do Brasil.* 12th ed. Rio de Janeiro: José Olympio, 1978.

Ianni, Octávio. "Relações de produção e proletariado rural." In Szmrecsányi and Queda, ed. *Vida rural e mudança social,* 148–59.

Iglésias, Francisco. *História e ideologia.* São Paulo: Perspectiva, 1971.

———. "Modernismo: uma reverificação da inteligência nacional." In Ávila, ed., *O Modernismo,* 13–26.

Johnson, Randal. "Authoritarian Fiction: Octavio de Faria's *Tragédia burguesa.*" *Ideologies and Literature* 3:1 (1988): 159–78.

———. "Brazilian Modernism: The Politics of Cultural Nationalism." Mimeo, 1988.

———. "Carta." 24 Jan. 1989.

———. "The Dynamics of the Brazilian Literary Field, 1930–1945." Mimeo, 1989.

———. "Modernism and Authoritarianism in Brazil." XIV Congress of the Latin American Studies Association. New Orleans, 1988.

Kundera, Milan. "O fim do tempo do romance." *Leia* VII, 74 (1984): 12–13.

Lafetá, João Luiz. *Figuração da intimidade.* São Paulo: Martins Fontes, 1986.

———. *1930: a crítica e o Modernismo.* São Paulo: Duas Cidades, 1974.

Lamounier, Bolivar. "Formação de um pensamento político autoritário na Primeira República. Uma interpretação." In Fausto, ed., *História geral da civilização brasileira,* tomo III, vol. 2, 343–73.

Leal, Victor Nunes. *Coronelismo, enxada e voto.* 4th ed. São Paulo: Alfa-Omega, 1978.

Leite, Dante Moreira. *O caráter nacional brasileiro.* 2d ed. São Paulo: Pioneira, 1969.

Lima, Luiz Costa. "Carlos Drummond de Andrade: memória e ficção." In *Dispersa demanda,* 159–75. Rio de Janeiro: Francisco Alves, 1981.

———. "Da existência precária: o sistema intelectual no Brasil." In *Dispersa demanda,* 3–29.

———. "José Lins do Rego." In Afrânio Coutinho, ed., *A literatura no Brasil,* 2d ed., 5:283–304. Rio de Janeiro: Sul-Americana, 1970.

———. *Lira e antilira.* Rio de Janeiro: Civilização Brasileira, 1968.

———. *A perversão do trapezista.* Rio de Janeiro: Imago, 1976.

———. "As projeções do ideológico." *Cadernos da PUC* 26 (1975): 155–203.

Lopes, José Sérgio Leite. "Relações de parentesco e de propriedade nos romances do 'ciclo da cana' de José Lins do Rego." In Gilberto Velho, ed., *Arte e sociedade,* 64–87. Rio de Janeiro: Zahar, 1977.

Machado, Dyonelio. *Os ratos.* 6th ed. São Paulo: Ática, 1979.

Machado Neto, A. L. *Estrutura social da República das Letras.* São Paulo: Grijalbo, 1973.

Martins, Hélcio. *A rima na poesia de Carlos Drummond de Andrade.* Rio de Janeiro: José Olympio, 1968.

Martins, Luciano. "A gênese de uma *intelligensia.*" *Revista Brasileira de Ciências Sociais* 2, 4 (1987): 65–87.

Martins, Wilson. *A literatura brasileira—Modernismo.* Vol. 6. 5th ed. São Paulo: Cultrix, 1977.

Medeiros, Jarbas. *Ideologia autoritária no Brasil (1930–1945).* Rio de Janeiro: Fundação Getúlio Vargas, 1978.

Menezes, Ulpiano Bezerra de. "Identidade cultural e arqueologia." In Bosi, ed., *Cultura brasileira—temas e situações,* 182–90. São Paulo: Ática, 1987.

Merquior, José Guilherme. "A estética do Modernismo do ponto de vista da História da Cultura." In *Formalismo e tradição moderna,* 77–102. Rio de Janeiro: Forense Universitária, 1974.

———. "Situación del escritor." In César Fernández Moreno, ed., *América Latina en su literatura,* 372–88. México: Siglo XXI, 1972.

———. *Verso universo em Drummond.* 2d ed. Rio de Janeiro: José Olympio, 1976.

Miceli, Sérgio. *Intelectuais e classe dirigente no Brasil—1920–1945.* São Paulo: Difusão Européia do Livro, 1979.

———. *Poder, sexo e letras na República Velha.* São Paulo: Perspectiva, 1977.

Miguel-Pereira, Lúcia. *História da literatura brasileira.* 3d ed. Rio de Janeiro: José Olympio, 1973.

Miranda, Wander Melo. "Repertório do clã." Mimeo, 1988.
Moraes, Reginaldo, et al. *Inteligência brasileira*. São Paulo: Brasiliense, 1986.
Mota, Carlos Guilherme. *Ideologia da cultura brasileira (1933–1974)*. 4th ed. São Paulo: Ática, 1980.
Mousnier, Roland. "A crise da consciência." In Maurice Crouzet, ed., *História geral das civilizações*, tomo IV, vol. 1, 4th ed., 218–30. São Paulo: Difusão Européia do Livro, 1973.
Multiple Authors. *Sobre o Pré-Modernismo*. Rio de Janeiro: Fundação Casa de Rui Barbosa, 1988.
Muricy, Katia. *A razão cética*. São Paulo: Companhia das Letras, 1988.
Needell, Jeffrey. *A Tropical Belle Époque*. Cambridge: Cambridge University Press, 1987.
Neves, Luiz Felipe Baêta. "A imaginação social dos sambas-enredo." In *O paradoxo do coringa*, 57–69. Rio de Janeiro: Achiamé, 1979.
Novaes, Adauto. "Apresentação." In Chauí, *Seminários*, 7–10.
Nunes, Benedito. "Estética e correntes do Modernismo." In Ávila, ed., *O Modernismo*, 39–53.
———. *João Cabral de Melo Neto*. 2d ed. Petrópolis: Vozes, 1971.
Ortiz, Renato. *Cultura brasileira e identidade nacional*. São Paulo: Brasiliense, 1985.
Pacheco, João. *O mundo que José Lins do Rego fingiu*. Rio de Janeiro: São José, 1958.
Pinheiro, Paulo Sérgio. "Classes médias urbanas: formação, natureza, intervenção na vida política." In Fausto, ed., *História geral da civilização brasileira*, tomo III, vol. 2, 9–37.
Prado, Jr., Caio. *História econômica do Brasil*. 24th ed. São Paulo: Brasiliense, 1980.
Prado, Antônio Arnoni. *1922—itinerário de uma falsa vanguarda*. São Paulo: Brasiliense, 1983.
Proença Filho, Domício, ed. *O livro do seminário*. São Paulo: LR, 1983.
Puccinelli, Lamberto. *Graciliano Ramos*. São Paulo: Quíron, 1975.
Queiroz, Maria Isaura Pereira de. *Os cangaceiros*. São Paulo: Duas Cidades, 1977.
———. "O coronelismo numa interpretação sociológica." In Fausto, ed., *História geral da civilização brasileira*, tomo III, vol. 1, 154–90.
———. *O mandonismo local na vida política brasileira*. São Paulo: IEB/USP, 1970.
Ramos, Graciliano. *Angústia*. 6th ed. Rio de Janeiro: José Olympio, 1953.
———. *Memórias do cárcere*. 4 vols. Rio de Janeiro: José Olympio, 1953.
———. *São Bernardo*. 29th ed. Rio de Janeiro: Record, 1978.
———. *Viventes das Alagoas*. 10th ed. Rio de Janeiro: Record, 1980.
Rebelo, Marques. *A estrela sobe*. Rio de Janeiro: Ouro, n.d.

———. *Marafa.* Rio de Janeiro: Ouro, 1970.

Rego, José Lins do. *Bangüê.* 11th ed. Rio de Janeiro: José Olympio, 1979.

———. *Eurídice.* 8th ed. Rio de Janeiro: Nova Fronteira, 1985.

———. *Fogo morto.* 13th ed. Rio de Janeiro: José Olympio, 1972.

———. *Menino de engenho.* 13th ed. Rio de Janeiro: José Olympio, 1968.

———. *Meus verdes anos.* Rio de Janeiro: Ouro, n.d.

———. *Plantation Boy.* Translated by Emmi Baum. New York: Alfred Knopf, 1966. 1–109.

Reis, Roberto. "Anotações sobre o Quixote." *Minas Gerais, Suplemento Literário* 931 (4 ago. 1984): 2.

———."O coágulo e a nebulosa." *Minas Gerais, Suplemento Literário* 906 (1984): 8–9.

———. "Os dentes do poema." *Letras* 29 (1980): 109–27.

———. "A fala impura." *Minas Gerais, Suplemento Literário* 700, 701, and 702 (1980): 2–4, 6–7, and 6–7.

———. "Fogos de artifício—anotações para o estudo do sistema intelectual brasileiro." Mimeo, 1989.

———. "A leitura como diálogo." *Correio do Povo* 19 ago. 1978. 12.

———. "Ler/dialogar—notas por uma teoria da leitura." *Minas Gerais, Suplemento Literário* 634 (1978): 4–5.

———. "O lugar da crítica e a crítica do lugar." *Minas Gerais, Suplemento Literário* 681 (1979): 6–7.

———. "Para uma sociocrítica ou pedagogia da crítica." *Chasqui* XIV, 1 (1984): 29–40.

———. *A permanência do círculo—hierarquia no romance brasileiro.* Niterói: EDUFF, 1987.

———. "Por uma crítica mestiça." *Rocky Mountain Review* 37, IV (1983): 183–94.

———. "Por uma teoria da leitura." *Revista de Cultura Vozes* 71, 10 (1977): 35–40.

———. "Tecendo a leitura." *Cadernos de Literatura* 13 (1982): 21–24.

Ribeiro, Darcy. *Teoria do Brasil.* 2d ed. Rio de Janeiro: Civilização Brasileira, 1975.

Saes, Décio. *Classe média e política na Primeira República (1889–1930).* Petrópolis: Vozes, 1975.

———. *Classe média e sistema político no Brasil.* São Paulo: T. A. Queirós, 1984.

Sant'Anna, Affonso Romano de. *O canibalismo amoroso.* 2d ed. São Paulo: Brasiliense, 1985.

———. *Carlos Drummond de Andrade: análise da obra.* 2d ed. Rio de Janeiro: Documentário, 1977.

Santiago, Silviano. *Carlos Drummond de Andrade*. Petrópolis: Vozes, 1976.

———. "A estrutura musical do romance—o caso Érico Veríssimo." *Boletim Bibliográfico* 47:1/4 (1986): 23–37.

———. "Fechado para balanço (60 anos de Modernismo)." In Proença, ed., *O livro do seminário*, 71–100.

———. *Em liberdade*. Rio de Janeiro: Paz e Terra, 1981.

———. "Vale quanto pesa." In *Vale quanto pesa*, 25–40. Rio de Janeiro: Paz e Terra, 1982.

Santiago, Silviano, et al. "Mesa-redonda." In Garbuglio et al., eds., *Graciliano Ramos*, 417–50.

Schwartzman, Simon. *Bases do autoritarismo brasileiro*. Rio de Janeiro: Campus, 1982.

Schwarz, Roberto. *Um mestre na periferia do capitalismo*. São Paulo: Duas Cidades, 1990.

———. *O pai de família e outros estudos*. Rio de Janeiro: Paz e Terra, 1978.

———. *Que horas são?* São Paulo: Companhia das Letras, 1987.

———. *Ao vencedor as batatas*. São Paulo: Duas Cidades, 1977.

Sevcenko, Nicolau. *Literatura como missão*. São Paulo, Brasiliense, 1983.

Silva, Hélio. *O ciclo de Vargas*. 16 vols. Rio de Janeiro: Civilização Brasileira, 1964–78.

Souza, Gilda de Mello, and Antonio Candido. "Introdução" to Manuel Bandeira. *Estrela da vida inteira*, 2d ed., l–lxx. Rio de Janeiro: José Olympio, 1970.

Souza, Laura de Mello e. *Desclassificados do ouro*. Rio de Janeiro: Graal, 1982.

Süssekind, Flora. *O Brasil não é longe daqui*. São Paulo: Cia. das Letras, 1990.

———. "O figurino e a forja." In *Sobre o Pré-Modernismo*, 31–47.

———. "Murilo Mendes: um bom exemplo na História." *Encontros com a Civilização Brasileira* 7 (1979): 147–69.

———. *Tal Brasil, qual romance?* Rio de Janeiro: Achiamé, 1984.

Szmrecsányi, Tamás, and Oriowaldo Queda, eds. *Vida rural e mudança social*. 2d ed. São Paulo: Nacional, 1976.

Teles, Gilberto Mendonça. *Drummond, a estilística da repetição*. Rio de Janeiro: José Olympio, 1970.

———. *Vanguarda européia e Modernismo brasileiro*. 4th ed. Petrópolis: Vozes, 1977.

Terra, Ruth Brito Lemos. *Memórias de lutas: literatura de folhetos do nordeste (1893–1930)*. São Paulo: Global, 1983.

Toledo, Caio Navarro de. *ISEB: fábrica de ideologias*. São Paulo: Ática, 1977.

Tolipan, Sérgio. "Sociedade e modernização—o Brasil dos anos 20." In *Sete ensaios sobre o Modernismo*, 9–12. Rio de Janeiro: FUNARTE, 1983.

Trindade, Hélgio. "Integralismo: teoria e práxis política nos anos 30." In Fausto, ed., *História geral da civilização brasileira,* tomo III, vol. 3, 298–335.

Vargas, Getúlio. *A nova política do Brasil.* 5 vols. Rio de Janeiro: José Olympio, 1938.

Vasconcelos, Gilberto. *A ideologia curupira.* São Paulo: Brasiliense, 1979.

Velloso, Mônica Pimenta. *Os intelectuais e a política cultural do Estado Novo.* Rio de Janeiro: CPDOC, 1987.

Ventura, Roberto. "Literatura e antropologia em Mário de Andrade e Darcy Ribeiro." Mimeo, 1988.

Veríssimo, Érico. "Ana Terra revisitada." In *Ana Terra.* Porto Alegre: Globo, 1971.

———. *O arquipélago.* Vol. 1, 9th ed., vol. 2, 9th ed., and vol. 3, 7th ed. Porto Alegre: Globo, 1979, 80.

———. *Caminhos cruzados.* Porto Alegre: Globo, 1934.

———. *O continente.* Vol. 1, 18th ed., and vol. 2, 20th ed. Porto Alegre: Globo, 1979, 82.

———. "O escritor diante do espelho." In *Ficção completa,* vol. 3, 13–174. Rio de Janeiro: Aguilar, 1967.

———. *O retrato.* Vol. 1, 13th ed., and vol. 2, 14th ed. Porto Alegre: Globo, 1979, 80.

———. *Solo de clarineta.* 2 vols. Lisboa: Livros do Brasil, 1973, 1975.

Walty, Ivete Lara Camargos, and Maria Helena Rabelo Campos. "As sete faces de um texto." *O Eixo e a Roda* 4 (1985): 78–87.

Weber, João Hernesto. *Do Modernismo à nova narrativa.* Porto Alegre: Metrópole, 1976.

Wisnik, José Miguel, and Enio Squeff. *O nacional e o popular na cultura brasileira;* Música. 2d ed. São Paulo: Brasiliense, 1983.

Zagury, Eliane. *Cecília Meireles.* Petrópolis: Vozes, 1973.

Index

About the Author

Roberto Reis (Rio de Janeiro/Brazil, 1949) is Associate Professor of Brazilian Literature at the University of Minnesota/Twin Cities. He has published poems, short stories, and essays on literary criticism in Brazil, Portugal, Spain, the United States, Mexico, Guatemala, Argentina, Peru, Colombia, Germany, Japan, France, Czechoslovakia, and Venezuela. He is the author of a collection of short stories, *A dor da bruxa* ("The Witch's Pain," 1973), a novel, *A hora da teia* ("The Spider's Web Hour," 1982), and an essay, *A permanência do círculo* ("The Permanence of the Circle," 1987), and editor of *Toward Socio-Criticism* (1991).